# REVELATION IN RELIGIOUS BELIEF

**DATE DUE**

| | | | |
|---|---|---|---|
| | | | |
| | | | |
| | | | |
| | | | |
| | | | |
| | | | |
| | | | |
| | | | |
| | | | |
| | | | |
| | | | |
| | | | |

George I. Mavrodes

# Revelation in Religious Belief

TEMPLE UNIVERSITY PRESS
PHILADELPHIA

Temple University Press, Philadelphia 19122

Copyright © 1988 by Temple University. All rights reserved

Published 1988

Printed in the United States of America

The paper used in this publication meets the minimum requirements of
American National Standard for Information Sciences—Permanence of Paper
for Printed Library Materials, ANSI Z39.48-1984

Library of Congress Cataloging-in-Publication Data

Mavrodes, George I.
    Revelation in religious belief.

    Includes index.
    1. Revelation. I. Title.
BL475.5.M38    1988        291.2′11        87-26697
ISBN 0-87722-545-1 (alk. paper)

# CONTENTS

[v]

# ACKNOWLEDGMENTS

Much of the material in this book was presented first as a series of lectures in the Institute for the Philosophy of Religion (funded in part by the National Endowment for the Humanities) that was held on the campus of Western Washington University in the summer of 1986. I wish to thank Professors William P. Alston and Alvin Plantinga, co-directors of the Institute, for their invitation to me to deliver those lectures. And to the other participants in the Institute I owe a debt of gratitude for the lively discussions that followed the lectures.

The Center for Philosophy of Religion at the University of Notre Dame awarded me a fellowship for the academic year 1987–88. The final part of the work of preparing this book for publication was done during the early part of my tenure of that fellowship. I express my appreciation to the University of Notre Dame, and to the directors of the Center, for this opportunity.

Finally, a special word of thanks is due to Mr. Lou Case and Ms. Sherri Kononetz for their careful work in typing and re-typing this manuscript.

# REVELATION IN RELIGIOUS BELIEF

# 1

REVELATION AND SOME RELATED

IDEAS

The subject of this short book is roughly that of revelation, and its bearing on religious belief and knowledge. I say "roughly," however, because the concept of revelation may not be fully determinative of the field that I wish to cover. In the West, at any rate, it has been fairly common to divide theological thinking into two categories, the division being based on an epistemological distinction. These categories are natural theology and revealed theology. Basically the same dichotomous distinction is sometimes made, of course, in other terms, such as reason and faith, or nature and grace. Now, I want to explore, philosophically, a certain basket of possibilities—possible ways in which God might act that would have important consequences for religious belief and religious knowledge. These possibilities seem to me to have more affinities with revealed theology than with natural theology. Some of them, in fact, seem to me to be just what we—at least those of us who work within the Christian tradition—are likely to think of first when we think of revelation. But some others in that basket of possibilities fit under the rubric of revelation only with some tension and uneasiness. They do not seem, however, to belong to natural theology as that is ordinarily construed either. And part of the early argument of the book is to the effect that no simple dichotomous distinction is likely to be deeply illuminating in the field of religious epistemology.

With respect to the possibilities that I do consider, I will not be arguing, for the most part anyway, that God actually has acted in one or another of these ways. That project might be more suitable to a work in systematic theology. I will rather be inquiring principally into whether it is *possible* that God has acted in these ways, and into what the consequences of such action would be, especially the epistemic consequences. But I must confess that my choice of the possibilities to explore is, to a large extent, guided by what I myself take to be the actualities or probabilities of divine action in the world. And my own judgments about that have been formed largely within the Christian faith.

These possibilities I will group into three categories, or "models of revelation," which I will call respectively "the causation model," "the manifestation model," and "the communication model." Chapters 2, 3, and 4 are devoted, respectively, to these models—including, of course, some material on what I take to be their relations to one another. This chapter is an attempt to locate the topic of revelation within the broader field of the epistemology of religion, and to give an initial characterization of the three models that will occupy our attention in the succeeding chapters.

Having suggested that the concept of revelation might not provide a completely accurate characterization of the field I want to cover here, I should probably say a little more about my hesitancy on this point. My "pre-analytic" notion of revelation, growing largely out of my experiences in churches, in the reading of Christian literature, and so on, has the "feel" about it—for me, at least—that it fits what I call the communication model quite well, and the manifestation model moderately well. But it does not seem to fit the causation model all that well. In fact, it may well be that St. Thomas, for example, would have rejected the causation model entirely, as a model of revelation, and Locke might have rejected both the causation model and the manifestation model as well. Perhaps, therefore, we ought to say that whatever possibilities I am including in this third model, and even in the second, belong to a mode of divine action that is something other than revelation.

On the other hand, the causation model seems to me to have significant features in common with the other two, and to be related to them in deep ways. Furthermore, it seems to me that the religious and theological literature of Christianity has not provided us with any other widely accepted category into which the causation model seems to fit more naturally.

At one level, this is largely a matter of terminology that is not crucially important. We might in the end replace the "pre-analytic" notion of revelation with one that is "post-analytic" and more inclusive. Or we might introduce new terminology to cover this other mode (or modes) of divine action. But this will not be a major concern of mine here.

I do, however, want to explore at some length a suggestion about identifying the field of revelation by appealing to the dichotomy already mentioned, that between rational or natural theology, on the one hand, and revealed theology, on the other hand. What at least looks like roughly the same intended distinction is sometimes made by referring to general revelation and its contrast, special revelation.[1] And sometimes this distinction is made without any very special terminology at all. C. S. Lewis says in one of his popular books, for example, "We are not taking anything from the Bible or the Churches, we are trying to see what we can find out about this Somebody on our own steam."[2] Lewis does not specify here just what our own steam consists of, or how much steam we have, but he does seem to suggest that if we were to appeal to the Bible or to the churches for information about God, then we would have gone beyond where our own steam could carry us. Maybe, he suggests, we will have to do that in the end, but first let us see how far our own steam will take us.

No doubt this proposal reminds us of some more precisely articulated distinction in the theological or philosophical literature. Both Thomas Aquinas and John Locke appeal to a dichotomous distinction between faith and reason in discussing religious belief. In the *Summa Contra Gentiles,* Thomas says:

There is a twofold mode of truth in what we profess about God. Some truths about God exceed all the ability of the human reason. Such is the truth that God is triune. But there are some truths which the natural reason is able to reach. Such are that God exists, that He is one, and the like. In fact, such truths about God have been proved demonstratively by the philosophers, guided by the light of natural reason.[3]

And in *An Essay Concerning Human Understanding,* Locke undertakes "to lay down the measures and boundaries between faith and reason."[4] In the course of doing that, he says:

Reason therefore here, as contradistinguished to faith, I take to be the discovery of the certainty or probability of such propositions or truths, which the mind arrives at by deduction made from such ideas which it has got by the use of its natural faculties, viz. by sensation or reflection.

Faith, on the other side, is the assent to any proposition, not thus made out by the deductions of reason; but upon the credit of the proposer, as coming from God, in some extraordinary way of communication. This way of discovering truths to men we call revelation.[5]

Both of these philosophers (and, I think, many who have followed them) refer to some "natural" capacity or faculty of human reason—no doubt what Lewis called "our own steam." This faculty extends to some, but not to all, of the truths involved in Christian doctrine. Those further truths, which lie beyond the range of reason, belong to the realm of faith and revelation. If we were satisfied, therefore, with something like the analysis provided by Thomas and Locke, then we might also be satisfied with identifying revelation as whatever epistemic mode there is in religious belief other than reason.

We can, if we wish, insist on understanding the concept of revelation in this way, as a sort of "wastebasket" category, a category defined simply as the complement of some other category. But a concept of this sort is likely to be unilluminating and unsatisfactory, because it is likely to include too large a range of sorts of events or activities. And in fact, neither Thomas nor Locke seems to be satisfied with a purely negative characterization of revelation. Thomas, for example, says that the truths that exceed the power of reason are "proposed to man divinely for belief." And Locke connects faith with propositions that come from God "in some extraordinary way of communication." Both of these claims involve at least an incipient positive characterization of this alternative to reason. Where there is some positive characterization of the categories on both sides of a proposed dichotomy, however, there we may inquire as to whether there is reason to think that the dichotomy is exhaustive and/or exclusive.

I will argue that in fact this dichotomy is neither exhaustive nor exclusive.

In one sense, of course, both Thomas and Locke recognize

that their categories are not mutually exclusive. For both of them hold that God may reveal truths that are also attainable by reason. Thomas, in fact, appears to hold that God reveals *all* of the religiously important beliefs that are involved in Christianity, including those "preambles" of the faith that are also within the province of reason. And he holds that this is indeed fortunate, because the majority of Christian believers—being, of course, philosophically unsophisticated—would otherwise be unable to attain these necessary cognitive foundations of the Christian life.[6] Locke, for his part, explicitly says that "the same truths may be discovered, and conveyed down from revelation which are discoverable to us by reason, and by those ideas we naturally may have."[7] And his own example of this possibility is his claim that God might reveal the theorems of Euclidian geometry. Later on in this chapter I am going to follow Locke in appealing to some hypothetical examples of this sort.

According to both of these thinkers, then, there is a possible overlap between the realms of reason and revelation. And according to Thomas at least, revelation *completely* overlaps reason within the area of theological truths. Later in this chapter I want to consider whether there is some further way in which these categories fail to be mutually exclusive. But first I want to look at the other side of the question. Is there reason to think that reason and revelation constitute a set of jointly *exhaustive* categories for religious belief? Or could there be a religious belief, or even a Christian belief, that belongs neither to reason nor to revelation?

Well, why not? Why shouldn't there be some other way of acquiring such beliefs, or even three or four other ways? Is there some argument that shows that there are no other ways? I must confess that if there is such an argument I don't know of it. Thomas, Locke, and many others like them seem to me simply to restrict their attention and their discussion to these two possibilities, but they do not offer an argument that there are no others. Why not? I don't know. Perhaps no other options came readily to their minds.

Are there really some other possibilities? The fact, if it were a fact, that you or I did not readily think of any such possibilities would not be any very strong evidence that there are none. Or so, at least, it would seem to me. For it might be that we are simply lacking in ingenuity. Intellectual history seems to be full of instances of someone's thinking of fruitful possibilities that had apparently been overlooked by many thinkers before him. If anyone does think that reason and revelation exhaust the possibilities in religious epistemology, then it would be useful to have an argument to that effect.

In fact, however, it may not be all that hard to think of some alternatives. In addition to rational theology and revealed theology, for example, why should we not recognize a category of *fallacious* theology? By fallacious theology I do not mean a theology whose content is false. There are, of course, people who hold that characteristically religious beliefs—beliefs, for example, in the existence of something of a personal or quasi-personal nature that transcends the world of ordinary experience—are false. And there are people who are themselves committed to a religion, and who hold that at least some of the characteristic and important beliefs of *rival* religions are false. But even if some (or all) characteristic religious beliefs were false they would not constitute what I mean by a fallacious theology (or a fallacious religion). Instead, I mean a religious belief, or a set of them, that is *true,* but that is held on some fallacious ground.

Could there be such a thing? Well, why not? Think, for example, of Thomas himself. He certainly seems to suggest that a person might begin by accepting the "preambles" of Christian theology—such beliefs as that God exists and that He is the creator of the world—by faith, taking them over from the Christian tradition in which he was reared. And such a person might possibly later on convert these beliefs to a different basis, that of philosophical demonstration. Thomas, indeed, seems to think that such a conversion would be, in some sense, an epistemic advance. Such a person would have improved his intellectual life, and would have converted some of his religious views from belief to knowledge.

Thomas, of course, believed that demonstrations of this sort had actually been produced by some philosophers, perhaps even by pagans such as Aristotle. And since he himself put forward five such "ways" of demonstrating the existence of God, as well as a variety of arguments intended to demonstrate the unity and uniqueness of God, and so on, seems plausible to suppose that Thomas thought of

himself as someone who had converted his own belief in\
the preambles to this preferable and stronger foundation.
Let us suppose, then, that at the very least Thomas' own
mature belief in the existence of God was based on the five
ways.

Now, many philosophers have claimed that the argumentation of the five ways is deeply flawed. Some of those who
make this claim, of course, also hold that the conclusion of
Thomas' arguments is false. That is, they are atheists. But
these are not the people whose views I am considering here.
For there are profound critics of the Thomistic arguments
who appear to agree completely with the Thomistic conclusions. These are the *theistic* critics of Thomism, who
hold that the conclusions are true but that the arguments
are deeply fallacious. An influential contemporary critic of
this sort is Alvin Plantinga, who in *God and Other Minds*
undertakes an extensive investigation of the Thomistic lines
of argument and concludes that they are unsatisfactory.[8]

Now, assuming both that Thomas' belief in God was
based on the five ways, and that Plantinga is right in his
evaluation of the logic of those arguments, it would seem
plausible to hold that Thomas' theistic belief was based neither on revelation nor on reason. It would not be based on
revelation because its own, "self-conscious," basis is a
course of argumentation from alleged naturally appre-
hended facts about the ordinary world. And it would not be
based on reason, at least not in the way in which philosophers such as Thomas and Locke appear to construe reason in this context. For by reason they seem to mean a
*sound* procedure of argument—true premises and valid in-

ferences. So, in the scenario I am here imagining, Thomas' theistic belief would belong neither to revelation nor to reason. Of course, there are plenty of philosophers who do not believe that the Thomistic arguments are irremediably fallacious. But we don't have to make this point just by reference to Thomas. Even if his arguments should turn out to be sound in the end, it would be hard to maintain with a straight face that *every* theist who bases her faith on an argument has a satisfactory argument at hand for this purpose. Fallacies are so common in philosophy that it would be a remarkable theological fact if it were the case that no fallacious argument for the existence of God were ever proposed or relied on. So whatever may be the case with Thomas himself, if there is any substantial number of people at all who believe in the existence of God on the basis of an argument, then it would seem to be almost sure that some of them believe on the basis of fallacious arguments.

Now, presumably a belief that is based on some fallacious argument ranks low on some scale of *epistemic* values. It need not, however, be low on every scale of values. Pragmatically, for example, a belief held on a fallacious basis may be every bit as good—as useful, effective, and so on—as it would be if it were held on some epistemically impeccable foundation. There seems to me to be an interesting question as to what is the *religious* (salvific and so on) value of a true belief held on fallacious grounds. But that, I think, is largely a theological question not directly germane to my topic here, and I will not pursue it further at this time.

We do have here, however, in the possibility of fallacious

belief, a candidate for religious belief that may belong neither in the category of reason nor in that of revelation.

There are other candidates. Consider what I will call, for want of a better name, *illegitimate* belief. Again, I do not mean a belief that is false, or whose content is in any way unsatisfactory. The concept of illegitimacy, as I use that term here, is like that of fallaciousness in that it has to do only with some shortcoming in the basis on which the belief is held. Illegitimate beliefs are beliefs held on the basis of arguments that somehow fall short of what argument in this field should be. But these arguments are not fallacious—at least not in the sense that they involve any failure either of logic or of truth. Could there be arguments of this sort? If an argument is logically valid—for convenience I will speak only of deductive arguments, though this line of thought can easily be extended to inductive arguments, too—if an argument is valid, I say, and if its premises are all true, then can it still be somehow defective or weak? Well, perhaps so.

You will remember that C. S. Lewis proposed going as far as we could under our own steam, before appealing to the church or to the Bible. But he did not say just what our own steam consisted of, or how much steam we have. What is the answer to those questions? What is the legitimate steam for driving natural theology? In fact, Thomas seems to propose an answer for such questions, although I cannot say that I understand that answer. In the *Summa Contra Gentiles,* immediately after explaining that there is a twofold mode of truth about God, Thomas says:

> Since, indeed, the principle of all knowledge that the
> reason perceives about some thing is the understand-
> ing of the very substance of that being (for according
> to Aristotle "what a thing is" is the principle of dem-
> onstration), it is necessary that the way in which we
> understand the substance of a thing determines the
> way in which we know what belongs to it.[9]

And this looks as though it should mean that all knowledge
about a certain subject, and all demonstrative arguments
about it, must begin with an understanding of the "substance"—perhaps that is what is now sometimes called the
"essence"—of that thing. It seems, then, that the Thomistic
view would be that the legitimate steam of natural theology
would be an understanding of the substance or essence of
God.

Unfortunately, however, Thomas immediately goes on to
say:

> But this does not happen to us in the case of God. For
> the human intellect is not able to reach a comprehen-
> sion of the divine substance through its natural power.
> For, according to its manner of knowing in the present
> life, the intellect depends on the sense for the origin of
> knowledge. . . . Now, sensible things cannot lead the
> human intellect to the point of seeing in them the
> nature of the divine substance; for sensible things are
> effects that fall short of the power of their cause.[10]

Now, it would seem that the conclusion to be drawn from
these two claims—one claim about the principle of all natu-

ral knowledge and demonstration, and the other claim
about what the human intellect can achieve in the conditions
of our present life—the conclusion, I say, would seem to be
that there simply cannot be any natural knowledge of God,
nor any demonstrative argument about God. Thomas, however, does not draw this conclusion. In fact, he immediately
asserts what seems to be the exact *opposite* of this conclusion, saying that "there are, consequently, some intelligible
truths about God that are open to the human reason."[11]
(And just before citing the principle of all knowledge he had
said that, "in fact, such truths about God have been proved
demonstratively by the philosophers, guided by the light of
natural reason.") The most that Thomas seems willing to
concede on account of reason's inability to grasp the divine
substance is that "there are other [truths about God] that
absolutely surpass its power."

I cannot say that I know how to reconcile these Thomistic
principles with the consequences that Thomas himself professed to draw from them. So I cannot claim to get from him
any clear idea of just what is the legitimate steam for natural
theology, for a natural human knowledge about God. Some
of our own contemporaries, however, have undertaken to
provide a clearer idea about this on behalf of Thomas and
other classical natural theologians. Ralph McInerny, for example, published an article in 1980 under the title "On
Behalf of Natural Theology." He refers to Thomas' doctrine
of the two possible bases of theological truth, and his claim
that some philosophers, guided by the light of natural reason, have demonstrated the existence of God. McInerny
then goes on to say:

The notion of philosophizing that emerges from such discussions is this. No matter how arcane and sophisticated a philosophical discussion becomes, it is in principle possible for the philosopher to lead the discussion back to starting points which are available to any man in virtue of his being human. . . . However chancy arrival at the *terminus ad quem* may be, the *terminus a quo* is where each and everyone of us already is. That is why a theology based on natural reason must be able to show how truths about God are derived from truths about the world and depend ultimately on truths no man can gainsay.[12]

Add in a rather similar vein, Alvin Plantinga had said somewhat earlier:

What the natural theologian sets out to do is to show that some of the central beliefs of theism follow deductively or inductively from propositions that are obviously true and accepted by nearly every sane man (e.g., Some things are in motion) together with propositions that are self-evident or necessarily true. In this way he tries to show that certain pivotal religious beliefs—particularly the existence of God and the immortality of the soul—are rationally justifiable.[13]

Like Thomas, these contemporary philosophers claim that it is not the case that just any old sound argument for the existence of God will be satisfactory for natural theology. Unlike Thomas, however (and despite the fact that they appear to intend for their characterizations to apply to

Thomas and his colleagues), their formulations of the project make no appeal at all to such notions as that of substance, essence, the "what it is" of a thing, or any similar Aristotelian or Thomistic concept. In the McInerny-Plantinga specification of the requirements for natural theology these ideas are apparently replaced by the idea of *universality.* What is special about the premises of the successful natural theologians is not that they express the substance or essence of a thing, but rather that they are propositions that are known, or believed, by "nearly every sane man," just "in virtue of being human," and so on.

This is an extraordinarily restrictive requirement, much more restrictive, I would suppose, than that which Thomas himself apparently espouses. Understandably, opinions differ on whether there ever has been, or could be, any serious argument that meets this standard. The McInerny-Plantinga characterization of natural theology, however, is not the only contemporary attempt to describe that project. A striking contrast, for example, is provided by the description recently put forward by Terence Penelhum. "Let us look at what is involved in proving something; and more particularly at what thinkers who have tried to prove the existence of God, or have tried to prove the truth of certain Christian doctrines about God, have considered themselves to be about," says Penelhum.[14] He then undertakes a discussion of several criteria for success in proof, and sums up the results of his discussion as follows:

> We have a proof, or a successful attempt at proof, when we have a true conclusion in an argument which

begins with premises which are true and are known by the hearer of the argument to be true, which can be stated without stating the conclusion, and which either entail it or make it overwhelmingly probable. It is clearly also necessary that the hearer understand that the premisses support the conclusion in one of these two ways.[15]

And a little later on he adds that theistic proofs should not begin with premises "which one could not know to be true without knowing that God exists."

Now, it seems clear that Penelhum himself believes that this description identifies a cognitively significant project, one worthy of serious effort on the part of philosophers and theologians. He says, for example, that if an argument that satisfies these criteria is presented to a hearer, and that hearer rejects the conclusion of the argument, then "he is being irrational in doing so, since for someone in his position the conclusion has been placed beyond reasonable doubt." And he adds immediately that the conclusion "has been proved to him even though he rejects it."[16] It looks as though this is an understanding of proof and natural theology with which Penelhum himself is satisfied.

Penelhum, however, makes a further claim for this way of understanding the idea of a proof. He says, we remember, that this account captures what "thinkers who have tried to prove the existence of God . . . have considered themselves to be about." He suggests that when Pascal and Kierkegaard, for example, criticized natural theology it was *this* project that they were rejecting. And in his discussion of this critical interchange, it seems clear that Penelhum intends to include Thomas and other "classical Catholic" apologists among those who "considered themselves to be about" proving the existence of God according to these criteria. So there is here also a claim about the historical adequacy of these criteria, their adequacy to illuminate the work of these prominent figures in the history of philosophy.

Between the project described by Penelhum, on the one hand, and that identified by McInerny and Plantinga, on the other, there seems to me to be just a world of difference. The McInerny-Plantinga criteria for success require a starting point where "each and everyone of us already is," premises that are "obviously true and accepted by nearly every sane man." The Penelhum criteria, however, require of the premises only that they "are true and are known by the hearer of the argument to be true." Penelhum, in fact, seems clearly to hold that the premises need not even be believed by the constructor of the argument. She might formulate the argument merely as an exercise in logic, without herself supposing the premises to be true at all. But if someone else—the "hearer"—recognizes those premises as true, then there has been a proof of the conclusion.[17] The gap between the Penelhum criteria, on the one hand, and those of McInerny and Plantinga, on the other, seems to me to be enormous.

Now, so far as understanding the idea of a proof itself goes, I incline toward Penelhum's sort of analysis.[18] I can see no plausible reason for requiring that a proof begin from, or be reducible to, premises that are believed by near-ly every sane person, or anything of the sort. After all, every sane person knows a lot of things that are not known, or even believed, by nearly every sane person. In fact, almost everything that any sane person knows falls totally outside the ken of most sane people. And I don't know why the derivation of a conclusion from premises that I know to be true should not constitute a perfectly satisfactory proof of that conclusion for me, nor how I would be any better off, epistemically, if the premises happened to be known or be-lieved by nearly every sane person.

I can see, too, how criteria so disparate from one another might well give rise to quite different judgments about the feasibility of the project to which they are applied. After all, the stock of knowledge that is shared by nearly every sane person appears to be very skimpy indeed. I, at any rate, would not be at all surprised if someone who thought him-self restricted to that narrow point of departure quickly de-spaired of proving any conclusion of theological or re-ligious interest. McInerny, of course, claims that it can be done and that it has been done. Plantinga, on the other hand, seems much more pessimistic.[19] Initially, at least, I would find Plantinga's pessimism about this project much more plausible than McInerny's optimism. However, one need not at all have the same pessimism about natural the-ology construed along Penelhum's lines.

That still leaves us, however, with the historical prob-lem—the problem of how to construe the project of Thom-as in the *Summas*, for example, and of how to understand the criticisms of a Pascal and a Kierkegaard. But I am afraid that I cannot now make any substantial advance on that problem in the history of philosophy.

Suppose, however, that someone believes in the existence of God on the basis of an argument that satisfies Penelhum's criteria, but that does not satisfy the criteria of McInerny and Plantinga. And suppose, too, that it is McInerny and Plantinga who are right after all about what is required for natural theology. It would be true, that is, that "a theology based on natural reason must . . . depend ultimately on truths no man can gainsay." In that case it would seem that the person we are imagining would not have her faith in God on the basis of revelation, for, *ex hypothesi,* it is based on an argument stemming from ordinary knowledge, perhaps knowledge derived directly from ordinary sense experience. But neither would she have a theology based on natural reason, for, again *ex hypothesi,* her argument does not have what such an argument must have. But also, her argument is not fallacious in any ordinary sense of that term. Satisfying Penelhum's criteria, it has no defect of logic, its premises are true and known to be true, and so on. This would be a case of what I have proposed calling illegitimate belief.

The possibility of illegitimate belief does not, of course, depend on our assuming that McInerny and Plantinga are right about what is required for a theology based on natural reason. The same possibility can be generated by assuming that it is Thomas's professed criteria that embody the true requirements for such a theology. For again we can think of a person whose belief is based on a sound, non-fallacious, argument that does not satisfy those criteria. In fact, *any* characterization of natural theology that imposes requirements that go beyond the soundness of the arguments involved would seem to open up the possibility of illegitimate belief, a belief that belongs neither to revealed theology nor to natural theology nor to fallacious argumentation.

But whether there is anything *wrong* with illegitimate belief—that is another question that I will not pursue further at this time.

Now, so far I have been arguing against the adequacy of any simple dichotomy in illuminating the possible bases of religious and theological belief. I have argued, by developing a couple of examples, that the reason/revelation distinction does not seem to be exhaustive. There is still another example of this sort that I want to consider—what I will call "innate theology." But this sort of theology is in fact the subject of Chapter 2. I will therefore leave until then the question of whether it really is a sort of revealed theology after all. Before leaving the topic of the adequacy of the reason/revelation dichotomy, however, I want to say a little against that dichotomy on the grounds that reason and revelation do not seem to be mutually *exclusive*.

I have already mentioned the fact that Thomas himself holds that the preambles to the faith can be held either on the basis of natural reason or on the basis of a revelation

transmitted by the church. But we can also think of some
other possibilities. Consider, for example, what we might
call "Locke's scenario." Locke says:

> Reason is natural *revelation,* whereby the eternal Fa-
> ther of light, and Fountain of all knowledge, commu-
> nicates to mankind that portion of truth which he has
> laid within the reach of their natural faculties: revela-
> tion is natural reason enlarged by a new set of discov-
> eries communicated by God immediately, which rea-
> son vouches the truth of, by the testimony and proofs
> it gives that they come from God.[20]

In this picture of things, which Locke apparently thought
was the really important one for Christian belief, a person
believes a theological proposition because it has been
proved that it was revealed. Reason does not generate revelations, but it vouches for the truth of them "by the testimony and proofs it gives that they come from God." So far
as I can see, anyway, there is nothing inherently absurd
about this scenario: it represents a genuine possibility for
belief. At least if we assume that it is possible that God
might reveal a proposition, a claim that I expect to discuss
more at length in Chapters 3 and 4, it would seem that
there might be a proposition, $p$, which was revealed. But
then the statement that $p$ had been revealed would itself be
a proposition distinct from $p$, and a true one at that. And
why then should there not be a proof of this second, true,
proposition? If there were, then it seems that we would be

well launched into the kind of situation that Locke en-
visaged.

Perhaps, however, someone has an objection that goes
like this. Assume that God has revealed a certain proposition, $p$. And now someone makes the claim (a true claim,
given our assumption) that God revealed $p$. That claim is
also a proposition—call it $q$—and it is a proposition distinct from $p$. It is a proposition about $p$, perhaps about how
$p$ came into human intellectual life, or about how someone
came to know that $p$, or something of the sort. And the
objector goes on to assert that it is not possible that a proposition such as $q$ should ever be proved as a piece of natural
knowledge. If $q$—the claim that $p$ was revealed—is to be
known at all, then $q$ must itself be revealed just as $p$ was.
And if this is so, then it would seem that Locke's idea of
how reason might vouch for revelation could not be correct. So runs this objection.

The thesis, however, that propositions such as $q$ could
not ever be acquired as natural knowledge is not at all obvious. I myself do not know of any reason to suppose that
it is true. It would be useful if someone who does hold this
position could provide some plausible argument in favor of
it. As a beginning, however, let me suggest a purely hypothetical possibility on the other side.

There has long been a doctrine widely held within the
Roman Catholic church (and often vigorously rejected by
Protestants) about the infallibility of the Pope. This doc-
trine asserts, as I understand it, that when the Pope makes a

pronouncement in a special way—speaking about matters of faith and morals *ex cathedra*—then he is the recipient of a special divine grace that makes him infallible in these pronouncements. There is, of course, some difficulty in determining just what is the *ex cathedra* way of speaking, and just when it is that it occurs, and the whole idea of papal infallibility has recently been challenged within the Catholic church itself.[21]

But it is not my intention to enter at all into this controversy here. I mention it only in order to develop my own purely hypothetical scenario as a sort of friendly caricature of this doctrine. But I must emphasize again that this is only a caricature, meant to illustrate a possibility. It is not at all intended as a discussion of the doctrine itself.

The phrase "ex cathedra" means literally "from the chair," no doubt a reference to the bishop's ceremonial seat in the cathedral. For the sake of our caricature, let us imagine that there is an actual chair, in the papal palace in Vatican City, that seems to have a peculiar property. And that property is that whenever the Pope speaks while sitting in this chair, then he never makes a mistake. If he says anything that has a truth value at all, then it is true. And for the sake of our caricature we will assume that this applies to every subject matter whatever, and not only to faith and morals.

We can also imagine that there is a person, without any religious belief at all about revelation or anything else, who becomes interested in the phenomena associated with this chair. At first, this investigator takes no special interest in the religious and theological pronouncements that the Pope puts forward from his chair. He does notice, however, that when the Pope talks about other things in that same situation—about medieval Japanese history, for example, and about biochemistry, and about Mexican archaeology, and about Basque linguistics—then everything he says checks out as true. And he may notice further that when the Pope is not sitting in this special chair, then he does not seem to be especially knowledgeable about these topics, and he often makes mistakes. To this person, therefore, it looks more and more as though something very special happens to the Pope when he sits in his special chair. In whatever can be checked on the basis of natural knowledge he just does not make a mistake *ex cathedra.*

Now, we can imagine this investigator continuing his study of this phenomenon to any desired extent. He can continue to gather more and more and more evidence of this sort. Eventually, we may suppose, he concludes that there really is something very special about the Pope and that chair. The combination of them generates a special epistemic virtue that guarantees truth. He concludes, that is, that when the Pope is speaking *ex cathedra* in this literal way then he is infallible.

So far as I can see, if there can be inductive evidence for anything, then there *could* be inductive evidence for this conclusion, and this evidence could be built up, even over generations and centuries, to any desired degree. If this is not even a *possibility,* then it would seem that there must be something deeply defective about induction in general, and about the alleged knowledge that is based on inductive argumentation. But if induction is basically okay, then it seems that there could be inductive evidence, strong to any desired degree, that some proposition has been revealed. (The Pope might *say, ex cathedra,* that what he says on religious topics in that situation is revealed.) And since this seems to be possible, I have no philosophical objection to Locke's Scenario.

In Locke's scenario, however, both the revelation and the proof from natural knowledge seem to be essential to the basis of the belief. And this suggests that revelation and reason should not be taken as mutually exclusive categories.

Once we think of Locke's scenario, it is not a large step to go on to its mirror image. That would be the case of a person who believes some religious truth because it is revealed that it has been proved. Assuming that there can be a proof of a religious truth, according to some criterion or other, it can be true that $p$ has been proved. And, assuming again that a proposition can be revealed, it would seem that this second proposition (distinct from $p$ itself) might be revealed. If so, then again the proof in natural reason and the divine revelation would both seem to be equally necessary for the belief.

There is still a third way in which this same result might transpire. Some time ago I read, in a source that I have now forgotten, the statement that only a Christian would have thought of Thomas' five ways. I have no idea of whether this is true, but if it is true it does not show that the five ways are not satisfactory proofs of the existence of God, nor even that they are not suitable for convincing unbelievers that there is a God. For there is a difference between the cause or occasion involved in thinking of some argument or piece of evidence and the logical and/or psychological force of that argument.

There is a story, for example, about the chemist Kekulé, who first proposed the ring structure of benzene. He had apparently long been puzzled over what sort of geometric structure the benzene molecule might have, a structure that would be consistent with the proportions of carbon and hydrogen in it that had been established by analysis, and with the generally accepted valences for those atoms. According to this story, one night he dreamed of a snake that formed a ring by taking its tail in its mouth. The next day he worked out the ring structure for the benzene molecule. Perhaps this story is true, and perhaps it is also true that Kekulé would never have thought of the ring structure if he had not had his dream. It may also be a fact that he had evidence supporting the ring theory. In any case, it is practically sure that the dream and its snake are not, and never were, any part of that evidence. In one way, therefore, the dream may have been essential for the belief in this theory, but in another way the evidential support for the theory, if there is any such support at all, almost surely is entirely independent of the dream.

A similar linkage between revelation and reason might be more extended. Consider, for example, the following hypothetical example. Suppose (assuming again that it is possible for God to reveal a piece of information) that God reveals to someone that a certain bizarre mixture of herbs and spices would have a powerful curative effect on cancers. This person, we will assume, believes this revelation, and (having cancer herself) she brews up some of the revealed concoction and drinks it. The result is a striking remission of her disease. Understandably, she becomes an enthusiast of this treatment, urging it on acquaintances of hers who also suffer from cancer. She may even sell a little of the brew locally.

There enters now into the picture a cancer researcher, who becomes intrigued by statistics showing an unusually high rate of cancer remissions in this town. He interviews many of the survivors, and finds that the only significant thing that they seem to have in common is the drinking of this strange tea. He thinks it highly unlikely that this could have any effect on cancer. Still, there are the statistics. . . . So he conducts a small pilot study, using mice. There are encouraging results, enough to get a grant from NIH for extensive testing. These tests, culminating with controlled studies of human subjects, produce strong evidence, perhaps practically conclusive evidence, of the effectiveness of this combination of herbs and spices.

Now, we may assume, if we wish, that this researcher has never even heard the story about the original revelation. Or if he has heard it, he may put no stock in it at all, thinking all talk of revelation to be nothing more than a primitive superstition. His own belief in the effectiveness of the remedy, and the belief of those others who accept the results of his research, need have nothing at all to do with revelation. In these scientifically oriented people this belief may be based entirely on the statistical and clinical and experimental evidence—except, of course, for the fact that they would never have had the belief at all were it not for the original revelation. For it may well be true that if that information had not originally been revealed, then neither this researcher nor anyone else would ever have thought of testing this bizarre concoction.

This is, of course, a purely hypothetical example. So far as I can see, however, there is nothing impossible about it. What examples such as this one show is that there is more than one way in which a piece of knowledge, religious or not, may depend on a certain mode, such as revelation. On the one hand, a given person's belief may be generated, or sustained, in him by some event or achievement belonging to that mode. On the other hand (for at least one alternative), something belonging to that mode may be some sort of ancestor of a belief that is supported by some other mode. So even if no one but a Christian would have thought of the five ways, those ways may still be satisfactory demonstrations of the existence of God, and effective ways of generating theistic belief in unbelievers.

Still another variation on this theme is provided by what we may call "the Westminster scenario." The Westminster Confession of Faith says:

The whole counsel of God concerning all things necessary for his own glory, man's salvation, faith, and life,

is either expressly set down in Scripture, or by good
and necessary consequence may be deduced from
Scripture; unto which nothing at any time is to be
added whether by new revelations of the spirit or tra-
ditions of men.[22]

Apparently the Westminster divines, though they had a very
strong biblical orientation, believed that there were some
religious truths—perhaps even some that were so important
that they were necessary for our salvation and/or for our
conduct of the Christian life—that were not openly and
explicitly stated in the Bible. Instead, these truths were to be
deduced from the biblical information "by good and necessary consequence." And if we were to find ourselves actually
engaged in this scenario, then I think we would be hard put
to decide on which side of a dichotomous distinction our
intellectual activity belonged. For in this operation, both the
biblical statements and the good and necessary consequence
seem to be essential.

A variant of the Westminster scenario, perhaps not clearly envisioned by the fathers of Westminster themselves, is
one in which one deduces a religious truth from premises,
some of which are obtained from the Bible and others of
which belong to ordinary life and investigation. This too
would seem to yield a mixture of revelation and reason in
which neither element is dispensable.

I have argued now at some length that the distinction
between revelation and reason is neither exhaustive nor exclusive. In the first place, the categories of revelation and

reason do not seem to exhaust the domain of religious belief. For there appear to be cases (or at least possible cases) of religious belief—and maybe indeed of religious knowledge—that do not fit comfortably into either one of these categories. My arguments about this point have been conducted, I must admit, without my expressing a firm commitment to any one detailed analysis or definition of the concepts of revelation or reason. In some cases, the arguments merely call attention to the consequences, along this line, of our accepting one or another classical or contemporary analysis of these concepts—for example, that of Thomas or McInerny or Penelhum. In other cases the arguments depend on our "pre-analytic" ideas of what revelation or natural knowledge involves. In either case, I suppose, the arguments might be rejected by someone who was willing to commit herself to some alternative analysis that did not have the consequences that I have drawn out here. If an analysis of that sort is actually forthcoming, then we can consider its consequences and its plausibility.

In the second place, the categories of revelation and reason—considered again in a sort of intuitive and pre-analytic way—do not seem to be mutually exclusive. That is, there appear to be cases (or, again, possible cases) of religious belief or knowledge that depend both on revelation and on reason, and in which neither element is dispensable.

If my arguments for these two points are basically correct and persuasive, it would not follow that the categories of revelation and reason were not useful for thinking about religious epistemology. What would follow, I think, is that

no simple dichotomy—for example, faith and reason, revelation and reason, natural theology and revealed theology,
natural knowledge and super-natural knowledge, nature
and grace, general revelation and special revelation, and so
on—no simple dichotomy of that sort is likely to be satisfactory and illuminating for thinking about how people actually hold their religious beliefs and acquire their knowledge of religiously significant facts. For that project, we
would need a considerably larger and more complex battery of ideas.

In this book however, I will not continue to survey the
whole field of religious epistemology. I am focussing on the
idea of revelation, and on those other possibilities that are
most closely allied with it. And, as I said earlier, I will try
to organize my observations around three models or modes
of revelation—the communication model, the manifestation model, and the causation model. Let me conclude this
chapter by giving a rough characterization of each of these
three, along with something about the distinctions among
them.

The communication and manifestation models are the
easiest to characterize, with the contrast between them illuminating each one. Imagine four people who say the following four things:

(1) Sí, hablo inglés bastante bien.

(2) I've lived in Mexico for several years, and I can
speak Spanish tolerably well.

(3) Of course, I'm a native speaker of English.

(4) Hablo italiano tambíen.

Leaving aside for the moment the idea of a divine revelation, we have here the human analogues of the communication and manifestation models of revelation. The first person *says* that she can speak English, but she does not manifest that fact. She does not actually speak in English. The second person, on the other hand, *manifests* his ability to speak English, but does not say that he has this ability. The third person both asserts and manifests his ability to speak English, and the fourth person does neither.

As I am construing the communication model, it is closely tied to notions such as those of saying something, telling somebody something, asserting something, asking about something, making a request, giving a command, and similar illocutionary acts. The manifestation model, on the other hand, invites us to think of acts in which some fact is made available for perception and apprehension. A person who actually speaks in English on some occasion exposes his ability to speak English, and he makes it possible for his hearers to recognize and apprehend that fact about him. This manifestation is independent of what it is that he says when he speaks English. In fact, a person who says:

(5) I can't speak a word of English, and I have never had any competence in English at all.

manifests her ability to speak English just as well as does the person who says (3). Of course, the *content* of what is said in (5) is in conflict with what is manifested by the saying of it, while in the case of (3) the content of the assertion corroborates what is manifested there. Thus, we are likely to be puzzled by someone who says (5), but not by the person who says (3). This puzzlement itself is an evidence that, in addition to what is asserted in (5), something is also being manifested there, something that does not fit well with what is asserted.

Of course, many other things besides linguistic abilities can be manifested by human actions, and many actions other than speech acts are suitable for making manifestations. An athlete manifests her skill and strength on the playing field, a man may make manifest the fact that he is bald simply by taking off his hat where he can be seen, a woman may manifest her love by her attentiveness to her husband, and so on. All of these things can also be the subject of communication and assertion. The athlete can brag about her skill, the man can admit that he is bald, and the woman can say "I love him." But to say these things is not itself the same thing as manifesting the corresponding facts (although, for example, one way of manifesting one's love might be by saying "I love you").

When we think of the divine revelation in terms of the communication model, then we think of God as *speaking,* as *saying something,* or something very much like that. If we think of the divine in such a way that speech and similar notions seem totally inappropriate to the divine nature—if, for example, we think of the divine as being impersonal— then we will not be attracted by the communication model of revelation. If, on the other hand, we think of the divine in terms of personality, or something similar, then perhaps this model will seem to us to represent a real possibility.

When we think of the divine revelation in terms of the manifestation model, on the other hand, the idea of speaking, and similar linguistic notions, need play no part at all. Here we are likely to think of something like an *encounter* with the divine reality. The language we use to express our convictions about a revelation in this mode is likely to be drawn from the terminology of perception and similar modes of experience. It is in thinking of God's revelation according to this mode that people find themselves talking about *seeing* God, about *feeling* the divine power, about being *flooded* by the love of God, and so on.

No doubt there is much more to be said about these two models of revelation, and I will try to say some of it in the chapters devoted to them. But perhaps this is enough for now.

The third model that I want to consider—and it is the one that I have already said may not fit the general idea of revelation as well as might be wished—is that of causation. Suppose that we think of God as being powerful, perhaps even omnipotent. And suppose that we think of God as being the creator of the world. It would seem plausible to suppose that an agent of that sort would probably be able to produce psychological effects in human beings. In fact, it might well seem plausible to think that God could produce some such effects directly. Suppose, for example, that someone who has had no discernible theistic belief throughout his life goes to bed one night, and he wakes up in the morning with the firm conviction that there is a God who is the creator of the world. Could it be the case that God has caused him to have this belief, inserting it, we might say, into his mind overnight? It looks like the answer to that question should be "yes." At least, if we think only of the divine power, it seems as though an effect of this sort ought to fall within the scope of that power. This would be one example of what I am calling the causation model of revelation.

Now, this example may strike us as a little bizzare. But in fact there are several important philosophers and theologians who hold positions that are not very far from this one. This group includes René Descartes, John Calvin, and some of the contemporary "Calvinian" philosophers. I will say more about that in the chapter on innate theology and the causation model of revelation.

I will discuss these three models in an order that is the reverse of that in which I have mentioned them here. Chapter 2 deals with the causation model and Chatper 3 with the manifestation model, and in Chapter 4 I will take up the communication model.

# 2

## THE CAUSATION MODEL

In Chapter 1 I suggested that we might recognize some varieties of theology other than natural (or rational) theology and revealed theology. Or, to put the point in terms of the basis on which one might hold religious beliefs, we might recognize bases other than faith and reason. In that chapter I suggested, as alternatives, such possibilities as fallacious theology and illegitimate theology. In this chapter I want to consider another basket of possibilities that I will group together under the name "innate theology." I will also suggest that this might be construed as a special type or mode of revelation, what I have been calling the "causation model" of revelation.

I don't know of any extended and specific discussion of innate theology, as a distinct variety of theology, by theologians within the Christian tradition. It seems to me, however, that there have in fact been significant figures within that theological tradition who have held positions that really do amount to an espousal of innate theology. That is, they have held (in effect) that the intellectual or cognitive content of the Christian faith, or some important part of that content, is innate in human beings. Or, if it is not in the strictest sense innate, it has an epistemic status that is more or less like that of an innate belief. Among these people I would count, for example, Descartes, Calvin, and some of the contemporary Calvinian religious epistemologists. And maybe there are many others.

Perhaps it should not be surprising to us that there has been this strain in Christian philosophy and theology. It seems pretty clear that these disciplines have very often picked up elements and conceptual frameworks from one or another of the more general philosophical systems that have flourished in the history of Western thought. Augustine, for example, is often cited as a Christian Platonist, Thomas' admiration of Aristotle is evident in his writings, and so on. The theme of innateness as an epistemic category has recurred often in the general history of western thought. It would be surprising if there were not some exploration, by Christian philosophers and theologians, of the utility of this idea for understanding and systematizing the knowledge that is professed within the Christian tradition.

At least from the time of Plato, in the fourth century B.C., right on down to Noam Chomsky, in the twentieth century A.D., there have been thinkers who have claimed that there is something in human intellectual life that could not have been acquired from our ordinary encounters with the ordinary world. They have thus rejected the adequacy of any radical empiricism for an understanding of human epis-

temology. If that rejection is correct, then of course these
elements must have some other source. And one way of
accounting for them is to say that they are innate. Literally,
of course, this should mean that these features are in us
when we are born. They are part of our "original equipment," in the way in which hearts and lungs are also innate.
But some innatists might hold that innate ideas are more
like teeth than like lungs: we don't have them when we are
born, at least not in any readily recognizable form, but they
will develop "naturally" as a normal part of the maturation
of the human individual. And if we are not fully satisfied
with that analogy—well, there are others we might try. But
more of that later, as we go along.

Saying that something is innate, however, is not fully in-
formative as to the epistemic status of that cognitive item.
For this account does not yet explain just *how* this item is
innate. As we shall see, there can be more than one answer
to that question. But before following up on this point, I
want to discuss a general sort of difficulty that faces the
most common sorts of argument in support of innatist
theses.

These arguments, as I understand them, proceed in this
way. They begin by observing that there is something in our
cognitive life that could not have been acquired in whatever
we take to be the ordinary and uncontroversial way of acquiring cognitive contents. And therefore, . . . The difficulty arises in trying to find some appropriate suggestion to
follow that "therefore." Something very general, such as
"these elements got into our cognitive life in some other

way," really does fit plausibly with the "therefore," but it is comparatively uninteresting (though not entirely so). More specific proposals, such as "these elements are innate," are more interesting, but their connection with the premise is more problematic. Let me try to illustrate this dilemma, first with an analogy, and then with two examples from Plato.

Suppose that we have a machine, a vending machine for candy bars. One puts coins into a slot, and pretty soon the machine delivers a candy bar into an open tray. So this is an input-output device, and we can observe the inputs and outputs. How does this machine work? What is its internal structure? Well, we can take off the cover and look. But suppose that, for some reason, we cannot take off the cover. In that case, the machine is a "black box." Its mode of operation has to be inferred (or just guessed?) from the correlation of the inputs and the outputs. Suppose that this correlation is comparatively unproblematic. It seems to be simple and regular. Whenever the proper coins go into the slot a candy bar drops into the tray, and the candy does not appear otherwise. So far, so good. But just what is happening inside the machine?

One suggestion, no doubt the one that occurs to us first, is that the machine has an internal stock of candy bars, each one individually wrapped and all of them carefully stacked in a dispensing mechanism and poised above the output tray. Once having imagined this internal structure, we are likely to lose interest in this problem (unless we happen to be mechanical engineers). Of course, we realize that the machine must also have some additional structure, something like a rudimentary "program" realized in hardware, which connects the input of the coins with the output of the candy. But maybe that seems to us to be "merely a question about mechanics." For whatever reason, once we understand that the machine operates on a stock of candy bars we are likely to think that we understand this black box.

There are, however, several other ways in which the black box might work. Perhaps, for example, it contains no candy bars at all. Instead, it has a stock of ingredients for the manufacture of candy—bins of sugar and chocolate and so on. And it has a more complex program than we first imagined, a program for the manufacture of candy bars. When a coin is put into the slot, then the machine goes into operation. It cooks up a candy bar, wraps it in waxed paper, and drops it into the output tray. And why not? After all, the candy has to be manufactured somewhere. Why shouldn't it be manufactured in the vending machine?

We may, of course, have some resistance to this suggestion. But I suspect that this is because vending machines are not, so far as we are concerned, really black boxes, fully opaque. Even if we can't look into *this* one, we think that we know something about such machines in general, and about their level of complexity. But if we really are thinking about a black box situation, a situation in which we have nothing to go on except for our observation of the inputs and the outputs, then this second proposal seems to stand on an equal footing with the first.

Nevertheless, it seems to involve a much different picture

of the inside of the machine—much different, that is, from the first picture. In one of them, we imagine the candy bars sitting there in the internal racks, already shaped and wrapped. There they wait, fully real and tasty before the customer arrives, and when the coin in put in, then all that has to happen in the machine is the movement of a few levers to allow one of these pre-existing bars to drop out. In the other machine we imagine no candy bar at all. Maybe there is nothing in it at all that even tastes very good. There are just raw ingredients—sugar, oil, chocolate, and so on. We would not want to eat such things as they are. No candy bar exists until after the customer comes and puts in his coin. And in this second machine, the coin sets off an operation that is much more complex than in the first case. We would be less likely to dismiss this program as "merely mechanics."

Furthermore, we are likely to think—or I am, anyway—that if there really is a black box vending machine, then there must be some *fact* of the matter about what there is inside that box and about what sort of program it has for its operation. It must either be much like my first suggestion, or else much like the second, or perhaps like some as yet undescribed third possibility. Even if the inputs and outputs don't give us a way of deciding among them, these descriptions seem to identify real differences among possible devices.

As I've already suggested, these two are not the only possibilities. Why shouldn't there be a machine, for example, that contains neither candy bars nor candy ingredients?

When a coin is inserted in this machine it sends a signal to a warehouse, and it soon receives from the warehouse either a candy bar or a parcel of ingredients. This seems to be a picture much different from the first two. Of course, someone might say that this case is not really much different from one or the other of the first cases. Such a person would go on to suggest that in this third case we simply ought to think of the machine as being much larger, or more extended, than it first appeared to be. It should be construed as incorporating the distant warehouse as part of itself. So it really belongs to one or another of the first types, except that its storage area is remote. We can adopt this strategem if we wish. But perhaps we ought not to forget that the first machines, even if they contain their internal stores right there beside the input slot and the output tray, are also presumably stocked from distant warehouses. If we count these warehouses as parts of the first machines, then again they may appear to be significantly different from the third.

There is, however, a rather more interesting alternative possibility. Think of a machine that contains neither candy nor ingredients for the manufacture of candy, nor does it receive either of these things from a remote warehouse. Nevertheless, it turns out a candy bar whenever a coin is inserted. How does it do that? Is it a miracle? Not necessarily. And we need not suppose that this machine makes candy out of nothing. Instead, we can think that it makes candy out of coins. That is, it contains something like a cyclotron, in which silver atoms are rattled around until they turn into carbon, and in which copper atoms are transmuted into hydrogen, and so on. And eventually these things are cooked up into a candy bar. Of course, because we really do know something about vending machines, we are not likely to take seriously any suggestion that there is a cyclotron in the snack bar. But if we really were in a black box situation, then this too would be a live possibility.

For our purposes here, this case may turn out to be rather interesting. The reason is that in this case the output is more intimately related to the input than in the other cases. In the first cases we are likely to think that the fact that it is a coin that results in the appearance of the candy bar is not a very deep fact. It would require only a minor alteration of the machine to make it deliver a candy bar if a match stick were inserted instead of a coin, or if a button were pushed, or if the machine were kicked, and so on. The coin is merely a sort of "stimulus" for the delivery of the candy, and the candy itself seems pretty much independent of the coin. In the last case, however, the coin seems much more than a stimulus. It is that, of course, but it is also the material that gets transformed into the candy, and thus seems to be much more closely related to the output. Later on, I want to call attention to a sort of analogue of this possibility in the field of religious epistemology.

No doubt there are many other possibilities that we could think of, if we set ourselves to think more at length about vending machines. I'm going to satisfy myself, for the time being at least, with these few possibilities. As I said, I hope to return to these possibilities later on as analogues of our epistemic situation. But for now, let us turn to some early discussions of this topic in Plato.

In the *Meno,* Socrates has managed to extract a version of the Pythagorean theorem from a slave boy, by questioning him persistently about the areas of various squares. He then discusses the significance of this achievement with Meno:

*Soc.* What do you say of him, Meno? Were not all these answers given out of his own head?

*Men.* Yes, they were all his own.

*Soc.* And yet, as we were just now saying, he did not know?

*Men.* True.

*Soc.* But still he had in him those notions of his—had he not?

*Men.* Yes.

*Soc.* Then he who does not know may still have true notions of that which he does not know?

*Men.* Apparently.

*Soc.* And at present these notions have just been stirred up in him, as in a dream; but if he were frequently asked the same questions, in different forms, he would know as well as anyone at last?

*Men.* I dare say.

*Soc.* Without anyone teaching him he will recover his knowledge for himself, if he is only asked questions?

*Men.* Yes.

*Soc.* And this spontaneous recovery of knowledge in him is recollection?

*Men.* True.

*Soc.* And this knowledge which he now has must he not either have acquired, or always possessed?

*Men.* Yes.

*Soc.* But if he always possessed this knowledge he would always have known; or if he has acquired the knowledge he could not have acquired it in this life, unless he has been taught geometry. For he may be made to do the same with all geometry and every other branch of knowledge. Now, has anyone ever taught him all this? You must know about him, if, as you say, he was born and bred in your house.

*Men.* And I am certain that no one ever did teach him.

*Soc.* And yet he has the knowledge?

*Men.* The fact, Socrates, is undeniable.

*Soc.* But if he did not acquire the knowledge in this life, then he must have had and learned it at some other time?

*Men.* Clearly he must.

*Soc.* Which must have been the time when he was not a man?

*Men.* Yes.

*Soc.* And if there have been always true thoughts in him, both at the time when he was and was not a man, which only need to be awakened into knowledge by putting questions to him, his soul must have always possessed this knowledge, for he always either was or was not a man?

*Men.* Obviously.

*Soc.* And if the truth of all things always existed in the soul, then the soul is immortal. Wherefore be of good cheer,

and try to recollect what you do not know, or rather
what you do not remember.[1]

In this discussion, Socrates thinks it important to emphasize that he himself did not tell the slave boy about the
Pythagorean theorem: "Were not all these answers given
out of his own head?" And he wants to make sure that the
boy has never studied geometry in the ordinary way. "Has
anyone ever taught him all this?," he asks Meno. "You
must know about him, if, as you say, he was born and bred
in your house." And Meno replies, "I am certain that no
one ever did teach him."
So how does the slave boy happen to know geometry?
Socrates' answer is that "this spontaneous recovery of
knowledge in him is recollection." And a little later on Socrates advises Meno, "Wherefore be of good cheer, and try
to recollect what you do not now know, or rather what you
do not remember." The Socratic view then, at least in this
dialogue, is that this knowledge is in the slave boy in the
mode of a *memory*.
It seems, however, that nothing could be in the intellect
at a given time as a memory unless it was in the intellect at
some earlier time. It can't just start out as a genuine memory: the concept of a memory has an essential reference to
the past, and indeed to a past piece of knowledge. Socrates
seems to recognize this. "If he always possessed this knowledge he would always have known," he says, "or if he has
acquired the knowledge he could not have acquired it in
this life, unless he has been taught geometry." And he goes

on to observe that, "if he did not acquire the knowledge in this life, then he must have had and learned it at some other time . . . which must have been the time when he was not a man."

The Socratic picture here, as I understand it at least, is that the slave boy has geometrical knowledge that he could not have acquired since his birth in the house of Meno. This knowledge is in him as a latent memeory, which can be brought to consciousness by Socrates' questions. And the boy must either have always had this knowledge, time without beginning, or else he must have learned geometry at some time earlier than his birth in the house of Meno, at a time "when he was not a man."

No doubt here Socrates intends to appeal to a common human experience. Sometimes we are sure that we know something, that we remember it, that we have not forgotten it, and yet we are unable to call it into conscious memory. "I'll think of it in a minute," we say. "It will come to me. It's on the tip of my tongue." And often enough it does come to us, perhaps stimulated by some reminder that seems to have no logical bearing on the truth of what is remembered. I think that Socrates is suggesting that the slave boy's knowledge of geometry is like that in some important way.

We can compare this passage with another Socratic discussion, this one from the *Symposium*. Socrates is here making his speech in praise of the god of love, and he recounts what he says he was told by Diotima, the Wise Woman.

"These are the lesser mysteries of love, into which even you, Socrates, may enter; to the greater and more hidden ones which are the crown of these, and to which, if you pursue them in a right spirit, they will lead, I know not whether you will be able to attain. But I will do my utmost to inform you, and do you follow if you can. For he who would proceed aright in this matter should begin in youth to visit beautiful forms; and first, if he be guided by his instructor aright, to love one such form only—out of that he should create fair thoughts; and soon he will of himself perceive that the beauty of one form is akin to the beauty of another; and then if beauty of form in general is his pursuit, how foolish would he be not to recognize that the beauty in every form is one and the same! And, when he perceives this he will abate his violent love of the one, which he will despise and deem a small thing, and will become a steadfast lover of all beautiful forms. In the next stage he will consider that the beauty of the mind is more honorable than the beauty of the outward form; so that if a virtuous soul have but a little comeliness, he will be content to love and tend him, and will search out and bring to the birth thoughts which may improve the young, until he is compelled to contemplate and see the beauty in institutions and laws, and to understand that the beauty of them all is of one family, and that personal beauty is a trifle; and after laws and institutions he will go on to the sciences, that he may see their beauty, being not like a servant in love with the beauty of one youth or man or institution, himself a slave mean and narrow-minded; but drawing towards and contemplating the vast sea of beauty, he will create many fair and noble thoughts and notions in boundless love of wisdom, until on that shore he grows and waxes strong, and at last the vision is revealed to him of a single science, which is the science of beauty everywhere. To this I will proceed; please to give me your very best attention:

"He who has been instructed thus far in the things of love, and who has learned to see the beautiful in due order and succession, when he comes toward the end will suddenly perceive a nature of wondrous beauty (and this, Socrates, is the final cause of all our former toils)—a nature which in the first place is everlasting, not growing or decaying, or waxing or waning; secondly, not fair in one point of view and foul in another, or at one time or in one relation or at one place fair, at another time or in another relation or at another place foul, as if fair to some and foul to others, or in the likeness of a face or hands or any other part of the bodily frame, or in any form of speech or knowledge, or existing in any other being, as for example, in an animal, or in heaven, or in earth, or in any other place; but beauty absolute, separate, simple, and everlasting, which without diminution and without increase, or any change, is imparted to the ever-growing and perishing beauties of all other beings. He who from these ascending under the influence of true love, begins to perceive that beauty, is not far from the end. And the

true order of going, or being led by another, to the
things of love, is to begin from the beauties of earth
and mount upwards for the sake of that other beauty,
using these as steps only, and from one going on to
two, and from two to all fair forms, and from fair
forms to fair practices, and from fair practices to fair
notions, until from fair notions he arrives at the notion
of absolute beauty, and at last knows what the essence
of beauty is. This, my dear Socrates," said the stranger
of Mantinea, "is that life above all others which man
should live, in the contemplation of beauty absolute."[2]

In this passage Socrates speaks of the apprehension of
something that apparently is not to be found at all in the
ordinary world, the world of ordinary experience. This is
"beauty absolute, separate, simple, and everlasting." It is
"the true beauty—the divine beauty, I mean, pure and clear
and unalloyed, not infected with the pollutions of the flesh
and all the colours and vanities of mortal life."[3] And this
beauty is not to be found "in the likeness of a face or hands
or any other part of the bodily frame, or in any form of
speech or knowledge, or existing in any other being, as for
example, in an animal, or in heaven, or in earth, or in any
other place."
So how does one apprehend something that is absolute,
everlasting, and unchanging, something not to be found in
any creature, whether in heaven, or in earth, or anywhere
else? Armed with the ideas of the *Meno,* we can provide an
account of this. The idea of absolute beauty is in us as a

latent memory, which can be brought to consciousness by the "hints" of beauty in the imperfectly beautiful things of this world. And since this is a memory, either this idea must have always been in us, without any beginning, or else we acquired it at a time prior to our entrance into this world of change and sensation, before we were infected with the pollutions of the flesh and all the colours and vanities of mortal life.

As I say, we could import into the *Symposium* this Platonic or Socratic account from the *Meno*. But what Socrates actually says in *this* dialogue, the *Symposium*, seems to me to make no use of those ideas at all. There is nothing here about memory or recollection, and nothing about the possibility of one's learning about absolute beauty at a time "when he was not a man." In this dialogue the cognitive order, the order of learning, is quite different. The process is one of "ascending" from the grossly imperfect to the less imperfect, and it culminates in a sudden *perception,* not a recollection. One learns first to appreciate the corporeal beauty of a single body, then of all bodies, then of institutions and laws, and so on. And after a long preparation of this sort, then, Socrates says, "he who has been instructed thus far in the things of love, and who has learned to see the beautiful in due order and succession, when he comes toward the end will suddenly perceive a nature of wondrous beauty."

What the comparison of these Platonic dialogues suggests, I think, is that Plato himself recognized that black box speculations allow for a variety of possibilities. Assuming that there is indeed something in the intellect that could not have been derived from the ordinary experience of the ordinary world, how could that come about? Where could that intellectual item have come from? Well, for one thing, it might be in the intellect as a memory. And that, in turn, allows for two further possibilities. It might be a memory of what was known at a previous time, which was itself a memory of a still prior knowledge, and so on back without beginning. Or it might be a memory of something that was acquired—learned, that is—in some previous state of existence when one was in contact with a different world. On the other hand, perhaps what the surprising intellectual content shows is that it is possible *now,* in the present life, to have an experience—a perception—that puts one in contact with another level of reality. Plato, I say, seems to recognize all of these possibilities. And there are no doubt still others.

Now, as I said earlier, there have been a number of theologians and philosophers who have held views about certain cognitive elements of religious faith, views that seem to fall into the same bag as those that we have just seen Plato exploring. Think, for example, of Descartes' observations in the third meditation. He focusses there initially not on a belief or piece of knowledge, but rather on a certain concept. He says that he has a concept of God—"a substance infinite, [eternal, immutable], independent, all-knowing, all-powerful, and by which I myself, and every other thing that exists, if any such there be, were created." And of this concept he says:

There remains only the inquiry as to the way in which I received this idea from God; for I have not drawn it from the senses, nor is it even presented to me unexpectedly, as is usual with the ideas of sensible objects, when these are presented or appear to be presented to the external organs of the senses; it is not even a pure production or fiction of my mind, for it is not in my power to take from or add to it; and consequently there but remains the alternative that it is innate, in the same way as is the idea of myself. And, in truth, it is not to be wondered at that God, at my creation, implanted this idea in me, that it might serve, as it were, for the mark of the workman impressed on his work.[4]

Now as I said, the concept of God, even if it is innate, is not itself the knowledge that there is a God, or any very similar piece of knowledge. Nor did Descartes think that it was. Consequently, in this meditation he generates an *argument* for the existence of God. And there may be something of interest and importance in exploring the relation between Descartes' ideas about the origin of his concept of God and his argument for the real existence of God.

His argument here, it seems to me, belongs to the class of cosmological arguments. The core of such arguments is that there is some observable feature of the world that is such that it could not exist (or, in probabilistic versions, that it probably would not exist) if it were not created and conserved by God. In Descartes' argument, the crucial feature of the world is a psychological fact, the fact that De-

scartes has the concept of God. For, Descartes claims, that
concept is so special that he could not possibly have it at all
if it were not produced in him by God Himself.

Why couldn't Descartes have made up the concept of
God for himself, or why couldn't it have been generated in
him by some other entity? Descartes considers these possibilities, and gives an argument against them. His argument depends on a puzzling principle, which appears in his
argument both in a general and a more specific form. What
Descartes himself says about this goes as follows:

> Now, it is manifest by the natural light that there must
> at least be as much reality in the efficient and total
> cause as in its effect; for whence can the effect draw its
> reality if not from its cause: and how could the cause
> communicate to it this reality unless it possessed it in
> itself? And hence it follows, not only that what is can-
> not be produced by what is not, but likewise that the
> more perfect,—in other words, that which contains in
> itself more reality,—cannot be the effect of the less per-
> fect and this is not only evidently true of those effects,
> whose reality is actual or formal, but likewise of ideas,
> whose reality is only considered as objective. Thus, for
> example, the stone that is not yet in existence, not only
> cannot now commence to be, unless it be produced by
> that which possesses in itself, formally or eminently,
> all that enters into its composition, [in other words, by
> that which contains in itself the same properties that
> are in the stone, or others superior to them]; and heat

can only be produced in a subject that was before de-
void of it, by a cause that is of an order [degree or
kind], at least as perfect as heat; and so of others. But
further, even the idea of the heat, or of the stone, cannot exist in me unless it be put there by a cause that
contains, at least, as much reality as I conceive existent
in the heat or in the stone: for, although that cause
may not transmit into my idea anything of its actual or
formal reality, we ought not on this account to imagine that it is less real; but we ought to consider that,
[as every idea is a work of the mind], its nature is such
as of itself to demand no other formal reality than that
which it borrows from our consciousness, of which it
is but a mode, [that is, a manner or way of thinking].
But in order that an idea may contain this objective
reality rather than that, it must doubtless derive it
from some cause in which is found at least as much
formal reality as the idea contains of objective; for, if
we suppose that there is found in an idea anything
which was not in its cause, it must of course derive this
from nothing. But, however imperfect may be the
mode of existence by which a thing is objectively [or
by representation] in the understanding by its idea, we
certainly cannot, for all that, allege that this mode of
existence is nothing, nor, consequently that the idea
owes its origin to nothing. Nor must it be imagined
that, since the reality which is considered in these is
only objective, the same reality need not be formally
(actually) in the causes of these ideas, but only objec-

tively: for, just as the mode of existing objectively belongs to ideas by their peculiar nature, so likewise the
mode of existing formally appertains to the causes of
these ideas (at least to the first and principal), by their
peculiar nature. And although an idea may give rise to
another idea, this regress cannot, nevertheless, be infinite; we must in the end reach a first idea, the cause of
which is, as it were, the archetype in which all the reality [or perfection] that is found objectively [or by rep-
resentation] in these ideas is contained formally [and
in act]. I am thus clearly taught by the natural light
that ideas exist in me as pictures or images, which may
in truth readily fall short of the perfection of the objects from which they are taken, but can never contain
anything greater or more perfect.[5]

In its general form the Cartesian principle here may be
stated as follows:
(D1) A cause must have at least as much reality as its effect.
This principle seems to appeal to the idea of degrees of
reality, which is itself a somewhat obscure notion. I have
elsewhere tried to make what sense I could of this idea,
relating it to the idea of ontological dependence.[6] Briefly, it
seems intuitively right to think that the dagger with which
Macbeth murdered the king of Scotland had more reality to
it than the dagger that he saw floating in the air. For the
latter, we think, was only hallucinatory. But Macbeth himself (along with his murder weapon) would seem to be less
real than Shakespeare and ourselves, for compared with us

he is only imaginary, a fictional character. Well, if there is anything to this at all, then we can think of a hierarchy of reality, level upon level. And God, if He indeed exists as He is described in Christian theology, would seem to belong to the higest level. For the existence of other things would depend upon Him, and not vice versa.

Assuming that we can make some sense out of levels or degrees of reality, principle (D1) has a good bit of plausibility about it. Or so, at least, it seems to me. A cause wouldn't seem to have enough "punch" in it to produce an effect having more reality than that cause itself. Maybe we can think of it this way. There are sometimes legal proceedings to determine the true paternity of some baby. And in these proceedings there are arguments intended to show that this man, or that man, or some other man, is the true father. There are also controversies like this, and the corresponding arguments, in works of fiction, arguments about the paternity of fictional characters. But hardly anyone, I think, would take seriously the suggestion that a fictional character might be the true father of some "real" baby. In a similar way, we would resist the suggestion that a fictional arsonist, no matter how clever, could have burned *my* house, the house I lived in. Maybe our reluctance to countenance these possibilities represents something of the appeal of principle (D1).

(D1), however, is apparently not sufficient for Descartes' argument. He needs a more specific version, which can be stated as:

(D2) The cause of a concept must have at least as much
        formal reality as the concept has of objective reality.

Formal reality, as I understand it anyway, is just "ordinary" reality. It is the sort of reality in virtue of which Shakespeare is more real than Macbeth. And God, if He exists, will in a similar way have more formal reality than Shakespeare.

Objective reality is more difficult. It looks as though a concept is supposed to have the same level of objective reality that its intentional object would have of formal reality, if that object existed. So if we can think of a hierarchy of entities, such as Macbeth, Shakespeare, and God, ordered in terms of ontological dependence and hence ordered in terms of formal reality, then there will be a parallel hierarchy of the concepts of those entities, with the corresponding degrees of objective reality.

If this is the right way to understand (D2), then it seems to be much more puzzling and problematic than (D1). In effect, it requires that the cause of Descartes' having a certain concept must have as much reality (formal) as would be required for it to be the cause of the existence of the object of that concept. That does not strike me as at all obvious. Descartes says that (D1) is "manifest by the natural light" and that (D2) is taught "by the natural light."[7] It seems to me, at the very least, that the natural light is a good bit stronger in one of these cases than the other.

Given (D2), however, Descartes' further argument seems fairly straightforward. He has a concept whose objective reality (since its intentional object is God) exceeds the formal reality of Descartes himself. Hence Descartes cannot have generated this concept "on his own steam." He doesn't have enough steam of his own. For a similar reason, this concept cannot have been produced in Descartes by his parents, or any other being in the ordinary world. In fact, since nothing other than God could exist that would have a degree of formal reality that would correspond to the objective reality of Descartes' concept of God, nothing other than God could be the cause of his having this concept.

Now, in this discussion we can distinguish two Cartesian theses. One of these is embodied in Descartes' argument for God's existence, based on the fact that Descartes is in possession of the concept of God. The other thesis is the claim that the concept of God is innate in him. These two theses are logically independent. The argument depends on Descartes' *possession* of the concept of God, but it does not in any way depend on that concept's being *innate*, at least in any strict sense. The argument requires that God be the cause of Descartes' having the concept, but it is completely neutral about *how* God causes that effect. If God, "at my creation, implanted this idea in me," as Descartes himself claims, that would be sufficient to satisfy his argument. But it would work equally well if God had implanted the idea when Descartes was fifteen years old. And so also would it work if Descartes, as an adult, had an "encounter" with God and a "sudden perception" (to use Plato's language) from which he derived the concept of God. The argument, therefore, does not require the innateness of the idea.

The innateness of the idea does not require the argument either. Even if we suppose that (D2) is false, or that Descartes' argument is otherwise fallacious, he might even so be right in his claim that his concept of God is innate in him. For that is not a claim about what follows from the fact that Descartes has this concept, but a claim about how he happens to have it.

Well, Descartes' theory about the concept of God is the analogue of the first of my speculations about the candy machine. He claims that his intellect came into existence— "at my creation," as he says—already stocked with the concept of God. Let us look at another theory that is the analogue of a different speculation.

In some recent work, Nicholas Wolterstorff has attributed to John Calvin a view of the sort that I have in mind here. Wolterstorff writes:

> What the Reformed person would suspect as operative in this and other cases of unbelief is not so much insufficient awareness of the evidence, as it is *resistance* to the available evidence. Calvin's thought, for example— which he bases in part on Romans 1—is that God has planted in every human being a disposition to believe in the existence of a divine Creator, and that this disposition is triggered, or activated, by our awareness of the richly complex design of the cosmos and of ourselves. It was not Calvin's thought that we *inferred* the existence of a divine Creator from perceptual knowledge of the existence of design. It was rather his thought that the awareness of the design immediately causes the belief— just as having certain sensations immediately convinces us that we are in the presence of another human person.[8]

Here the claim is not that God has directly implanted in us an idea of Himself, whether at our creation or at any other time, or that He has directly implanted in us any belief about Himself. What He has done, according to this view, is to implant in the human intellect a natural disposition to generate the belief that there is a God, a disposition that will be activated by any one of a variety of possible stimuli involving perceptions of the natural world. One such possible stimulus, for example, would be the experience of seeing the blazing beauty of the sky on a clear night.

Of course, there have been many philosophers who have professed to *infer* the existence of God from striking natural phenomena, such as the starry heavens above. Wolterstorff, for the most part at least, holds that Calvin is not claiming that we make such an inference. He is, rather, defending a *non-inferential* knowledge of the existence of God, or at least a non-inferential belief in God.

Now, it certainly seems possible that, if there is a God, then He could arrange things in the way in which Calvin and Wolterstorff suggest. He could create the human psychological and cognitive machinery with a certain "set," a disposition of the sort that Thomas Reid described, in this case a disposition to generate a certain religious belief on the occasion of a certain sort of stimulus. Or, for that matter, He could create human beings in such a way that *some* of them had this disposition. (After all, if God is the creator of human beings at all, then presumably He created them in such a way that some of them have blue eyes, some have brown eyes, and so on. Why should it be thought impossible that we should have some differences also in our psychological dispositions?) At any rate, if there is a reason for believing that it would be more difficult for God to give us a disposition of this Calvin-Wolterstorff sort than for Him to give us some of the other physical and psychological properties that we have, then I do not know what that reason is.

This view (the Calvin-Wolterstorff view) of belief in God is the analogue of my second version of the candy machine, the machine that manufactures a candy bar when a coin is put in the slot. In contrast with the Cartesian theory, this view does not picture the mind as being created with a ready-made stock of cognitive elements belonging to the Christian faith. Instead, the mind is created with a built-in "program" for producing those elements when it is appropriately stimulated. And as in the case of the machines, it is hard to see how one might decide between these competing pictures of how our cognitive machinery is constructed, if we are limited to speculations on the basis of the observed inputs and outputs.

Perhaps this is the place to insert two additional related observations. The first concerns a sort of reciprocity in our thinking about the cognitive life. At least in a rough and ready way we can distinguish two sorts of elements in that life. The first sort is basically that of a "content": beliefs, concepts, and ideas seem to be the best examples of this. The other sort of element is something like a "power," a disposition, a faculty, an ability, and so on. Here we can think of a power of abstraction, for example, or a power of inference, or of synthesis, and so on. This element is concerned primarily, not with what the intellect already has in its stock, but rather with what the intellect can *do*.

Now, empirical philosophers have sometimes used the

analogy of the *tabula rasa,* picturing the primal state of the intellect as a wax tablet, smooth and clean. But that picture can be interpreted in at least two ways. It is sometimes taken to mean that there are no innate ideas; the wax tablet contains no information, no beliefs, no concepts, until these are "impressed" upon it from the outside, presumably by sensation. The slogan for this view is, "Nothing is in the intellect that was not first in the senses." But the *tabula rasa* picture may also invite us to think that the active powers of the intellect are much like those of a wax tablet—that is, that they are very limited. The power of the intellect is pretty much restricted to the capacity to receive impressions (and perhaps to perform a few other elementary operations, such as combining parts of impressions and so on).

The friends of innate ideas, and their camp-followers, repeatedly marshall against this sort of view a battery of similar questions. How does the slave boy come up with the Pythagorean theorem? How does the lover finally apprehend the idea of an absolute, unchanging, and unblemished beauty? How does Descartes come to have the idea of a being with properties that infinitely transcend those of every sensible object? How do children acquire the grammar of their native language? This battery is powerful against what we might call "double-barrelled" empiricism, an empiricism that accepts both of the suggestions of the *tabula rasa* picture. For the output of the intellect seems to contain information—knowledge, concepts, ideas, and so on—that is simply not there in the sensible input.

The philosopher who is an innatist in the strictest sense—someone like Descartes, perhaps—solves this problem by claiming that the additional information belongs to the original patrimony of the intellect. The *tabula* simply is not *rasa* at its creation. It comes into being already inscribed. But such a philosopher can, I think, accept the other invitation of the *tabula rasa* picture. He need not ascribe any great powers to the intellect. (We may remember that the candy machine that has internal stock of candy bars needs only a comparatively simple mechanics for its operation.) For what is most interesting in the output is construed as being already there as a primal content, fully formed from the beginning.

Innatists in a looser sense (or maybe they should not be called innatists at all but something else)—people like Calvin and Wolterstorff—can accept the first invitation of the *tabula rasa* analogy, but not the second. They need not hold that we come already supplied with the crucial and interesting ideas and knowledge. Those things are generated, produced by the intellect, and indeed this generation may be provoked by our sense experience. But they cannot hold that the active powers of the intellect are pretty much like those of a piece of wax. For them, the intellect must be much more active, more resourceful, more creative, one might say. It has a disposition to go beyond the information that is logically contained in the incoming stimulus.

And is there still another way of responding to the innatist's battery of questions? Might a person hold that we have not yet identified all of the relevant inputs, that there is in fact a hidden input that provides the information that appears in the surprising outputs? No doubt there are some who do hold such a view. But that is the topic of the third and fourth chapters.

Here, however, we can take note of the reciprocity I mentioned above. It seems that in response to the innatist's questions we have a choice between enriching our view of the primal *content* of the intellect, or enriching the primal *powers* of the intellect. A cognitive black box that is rich in initial content might be correspondingly poor in power, and vice versa. But, at least without an appeal to the possibility of a hidden input, these elements seem to behave like a teeter-totter. As one side falls the other one must rise.

The second related observation that I promised above is this. It seems, to me at least, that the innatists must be right in some minimal sense. That is, there could not be a cognitive and intellectual life at all unless *something* were innate. Perhaps no one has ever seriously denied this. I suppose that even the most rabid empiricists, defending the *tabula rasa* epistemology, must have acknowledged that at least the *tabula* itself, or the disposition to generate a *tabula* as one matured, was a primal and characteristic feature of human beings. After all, if initially one did not even have the capacity to receive sense impressions, then the life of the intellect could not begin with sense perceptions. So if we do not have innate cognitive contents, then we must at least have some innate cognitive powers and capacities.

Perhaps, therefore, Descartes was right in thinking that the concept of God is "the mark of the workman impressed on his work." But even if he is wrong about this particular mark, if I have been created by a divine workman at all, then there is *something* in my intellectual life that He has impressed upon me from my creation.

Returning now to the Calvin-Wolterstorff view, so far I have been thinking of it in terms of a disposition that is activated by a stimulus. This invites us to think of the relation here between stimulus and output as adventitious, rather arbitrary. God, we are likely to think, may indeed have made the starry heavens the stimulus that will set off the disposition that generates theistic belief, but He could very well have chosen some entirely different stimulus instead. The button that sets this machinery in motion is pretty much on the periphery of the machine, and no deep change would have been required to replace it with something else. But in the case of the vending machine I put forward still another possibility—the machine that makes candy by transmuting the elements in the input coins—and that arrangement seems to make the input much more integrally related to the output. Is there a cognitive analogue of that speculation? Maybe there is.

Recently we have become accustomed to distinguishing between a cognitive stimulus *simpliciter* and a stimulus that is a piece of evidence for the belief that it generates. We have been invited, for example, to imagine cases in which a brain tumor produces beliefs—produces them, I suppose, by rubbing against nerves in the brain. Well, maybe that is a conceivable state of affairs. And if we can go this far, then I suppose we can take seriously the possibility that a tumor

might in this way produce a belief in the Pythagorean theorem, or in the proposition that the moon is smaller than
the planet Jupiter. And we are likely to think a person who
has these beliefs in this way both has his beliefs without
evidence and has them in a way that is low in epistemic
value.

A more curious case, however, is that in which the tumor
causes (in this way) the belief that the person himself has a
tumor. Maybe the person still has the belief without evidence, but it may not be all that obvious that his belief is
short of epistemic value. For in this case the belief and its
cause are intimately related.

Now, in the Calvin-Wolterstorff scenario the belief in
God is the output of a natural disposition that is triggered
by sense perceptions of the night sky and similar wonders
of the natural world. Is that an evidentially based belief? It
seems to me that Wolterstorff himself is ambivalent about
this question. Sometimes—maybe for the most part—he
seems interested in defending the propriety of this as a belief *without* evidence. He says, for example:

> Deeply embedded in the Reformed tradition is the
> conviction that a person's belief that God exists may
> be a justifed belief even though that person has not
> inferred that belief from others of his beliefs which
> provide good evidence for it. After all, not all the
> things we are justified in believing have been inferred
> from other beliefs. We have to start somewhere! And
> the Reformed tradition has insisted that the belief that

God exists, that God is Creator, etc., may justifiably be found there in the foundation of our system of beliefs. In that sense, the Reformed tradition has been fideist, not evidentialist, in its impulse. It seems to me that that impulse is correct. It is not in general true that to be justified in believing in God one has to believe this on the basis of evidence provided by one's other beliefs. We are entitled to reason *from* our belief in God without first having reasoned *to* it.[9]

But there are also times when he seems to say that a person who is in this situation has a lot of evidence for the reality of God, so much evidence that if he does not believe then it would be futile to give him any more evidence. ("What the Reformed person would suspect as operative in this and other cases of unbelief is not so much insufficient awareness of the evidence, as it is *resistance* to the available evidence.") And perhaps this ambivalence reflects the fact that we are not all that clear about just what makes something evidence for something else. Maybe, for that matter, we should have taken it to be a little suspicious that exactly the items that the Calvin-Wolterstorff scenario takes as the *triggers* for this disposition have been taken by a lot of other thinkers to be among the most striking *evidences* for the existence of God.

What is the evidential relation anyway? What is it that makes X a piece of evidence for Y? The detective observes a footprint in the soft soil beneath a window, and she comes to believe that someone stood outside that window, perhaps looking in. She seems to have evidence for that belief—maybe not absolutely conclusive evidence, but not inconsequential evidence either. What is it that makes the footprint evidence of the window looker: Is it just the *fact* that an indentation shaped like a human foot is very unlikely to appear in such a location unless a human being has stood there? I suppose that this is indeed a fact. But if a causal fact such as this one generates the evidential relation, then it would seem that either Christian theology is radically mistaken or else the starry heavens are very good evidence for God. For according to the doctrine of the divine creation and preservation of the world, the stars could not exist at all if they were not created and sustained by God. They are not the right sort of thing to exist on their own hook. Given this understanding of what evidence is, therefore, it seems that Christians should hold that the stars (and everything else) are evidence for God, and perhaps they should also hold that if the Calvin-Wolterstorff scenario is correct then theistic believers do have evidence for their beliefs.

Perhaps, however, we are inclined to think that a mere fact, or a thing, cannot be evidence for anything. Evidence must not only have a cognitive significance; it must itself be a cognitive item. (Perhaps this could be represented as a slogan, "Knowledge comes only from knowledge.") Evidence must itself be a piece of knowledge. According to this view, it would not be quite correct to say that the footprint was evidence that there had been a window looker. It is the detective's *knowledge* of the footprint that is the evidence. Until someone sees the footprint, and maybe until she has some belief or knowledge about it, there is no evidence.

Whatever may be the plausibility of this suggestion it can serve to make us notice that there are two ways in which we can understand the Calvin-Wolterstorff idea about the triggering mechanism for the disposition to generate the belief in God. Abstractly, at least, it would seem that a disposition of this sort might be set off by just about anything. God might have arranged that part of the machinery in any one of a great variety of ways. But maybe what Calvin and Wolterstorff have in mind is that it is some *judgment,* some *belief,* some *recognition,* or some other cognitive item that sets off the theistic believing disposition. No doubt the stars, the sea, the mountains, and various other aspects of the world affect me in various ways, and many of those ways give rise to no corresponding cognitive element. If it should happen, however, that the disposition to believe in God cannot be set off in that way, but only via some judgment or belief about the world, then perhaps we should say that theism is an evidentially based belief after all.

However that may be, we can say at least this much. If there is no God, then of course there is no divine revelation, whether by causation or in any other mode. If there is a God, however, then it seems quite possible that one way in which people might come to have the corresponding belief is that God simply *causes* them to have that belief. And that might happen in any of several apparently different ways. God might simply "implant" that belief, either from the very beginning of that person's existence or at some later time. Or God might instead endow the person with a cognitive "set" or disposition that will generate the belief on the occasion of a certain stimulus, and then God might provide the stimulus also. And this stimulus either might itself be a cognitive item—a belief, judgment, or some such thing—or it might be some non-cognitive item—a cosmic ray hitting some nerve in my brain, say—that had a cognitive result. Whether either of these cases should be counted as believing on evidence depends on the proper analysis of the concept of evidence. And whether any of these possibilities should be counted as revelation is perhaps merely a matter of a terminological choice.

# 3

## THE MANIFESTATION MODEL

In the preceding chapter we discussed the possibility that some important cognitive elements in religious faith might be innate, or else might have a status rather similar to that of an innate belief. If there are such elements, and if it really is God who (as Descartes says) "implanted this idea in me," then maybe we could say that these beliefs were revealed. On the other hand, we might prefer a different terminology for that situation, rather than speaking of revelation. However that may be, in this chapter I want to consider a somewhat different set of possibilities that seem closer to traditional ideas of revelation. These possibilities have to do with something like an *experience* of God, a sort of perception, or quasi-perception, of the divine presence.

The literature of religion seems to be full of testimonies and reports that fall into this general category. I am personally most familiar with such reports from within the Christian tradition and the pre-Christian Hebrew biblical writings. The examples that I cite here will come from these sources. But the literature of other religions is not lacking in some comparable testimony. I shall not immediately enter into a discussion of whether that fact constitutes a serious problem.

William James' Gifford Lectures, *The Varieties of Religious Experience,* now a little over eighty years old, contains a wealth of reports of this sort. Let me quote here just one of the many that James has collected and preserved in this book. James says:

> Here is another document, even more definite in character, which, the writer being a Swiss, I translate from the French original.
>
> "I was in perfect health: we were on our sixth day of tramping, and in good training. We had come the day before from Sixt to Trient by Buet. I felt neither fatigue, hunger, nor thirst, and my state of mind was equally healthy. I had had at Forlaz good news from home; I was subject to no anxiety, either near or remote, for we had a good guide, and there was not a shadow of uncertainty about the road we should follow. I can best describe the condition in which I was by calling it a state of equilibrium. When all at once I experienced a feeling of being raised above myself, I felt the presence of God—I tell of the thing just as I was conscious of it—as if his goodness and his power were penetrating me altogether. The throb of emotion was so violent that I could barely tell the boys to pass on and not wait for me. I then sat down on a stone, unable to stand any longer, and my eyes overflowed

with tears. I thanked God that in the course of my life
he had taught me to know him, that he sustained my
life and took pity both on the insignificant creature
and on the sinner that I was. I begged him ardently
that my life might be consecrated to the doing of his
will. I felt his reply, which was that I should do his will
from day to day, in humility and poverty, leaving him,
the Almighty God, to be judge of whether I should
some time be called to bear witness more conspic-
ously. Then, slowly, the ecstasy left my heart; that is, I
felt that God had withdrawn the communion which he
had granted, and I was able to walk on, but very slowly, so strongly was I still possessed by the interior emotion. Besides, I had wept uninterruptedly for several
minutes, my eyes were swollen, and I did not wish my
companions to see me. The state of ecstasy may have
lasted four or five minutes, although it seemed at the
time to last much longer. My comrades waited for me
ten minutes at the cross of Barine, but I took about
twenty-five or thirty minutes to join them, for as well
as I can remember, they said that I had kept them back
for about half an hour. The impression had been so
profound that in climbing slowly the slope I asked myself if it were possible that Moses on Sinai could have
had a more intimate communication with God. I think
it well to add that in this ecstasy of mine God had
neither form, color, odor, nor taste; moreover, that the
feeling of his presence was accompanied with no deter-
minate localization. It was rather as if my personality

had been transformed by the presence of a *spiritual spirit*. But the more I seek words to express this intimate intercourse, the more I feel the impossibility of describing the thing by any of our usual images. At bottom the expression most apt to render what I felt is this: God was present, though invisible; he fell under no one of my senses, yet my consciousness perceived him"[1]

James himself, in summarizing the significance of testimonies such as this one, says:

The whole array of our instances leads to a conclusion something like this: It is as if there were in the human consciousness a *sense of reality, a feeling of objective presence, a perception* of what we may call "something there," more deep and more general than any of the special and particular "senses" by which the current psychology supposes existent realities to be originally revealed. If this were so, we might suppose the senses to waken our attitudes and conduct as they so habitually do, by first exciting this sense of reality; but anything else, any idea, for example, that might similarly excite it, would have that same prerogative of appearing real which objects of sense normally possess. So far as religious conceptions were able to touch this reality-feeling. they would be believed in in spite of criticism, even though they might be so vague and remote as to be almost unimaginable, even though they might be such non-entities in point of *whatness,* as Kant makes the objects of his moral theology to be.[2]

In this passage James stresses the "sense of reality," the "objectivity," the conviction that one is in touch with "something there," that often characterizes such experiences. And he calls special attention to the fact that this is a feature also of ordinary sense experience. In this, James seems to me to be surely correct. A few of us may, I suppose, sometimes get ourselves into a skeptical mood about this element in sense experience. But most of the time—and, for most people, practically all of the time—we yield readily enough to the conviction that sensation puts us in touch with a real world, with a "something there," something that has its own career in reality independently of our experience of it. And James is here claiming that the religious experiences that he is here citing have that same feature about them. They too present themselves as putting the experiencer in touch with an independent reality.

The Hebrew Scriptures are full of references to the self-manifestation of God, but most of them have a somewhat different flavor from the experiences cited by James, and they seem to belong most naturally to the model to be discussed in the fourth chapter. I will give here just one example from this source, an incident in the life of the prophet Isaiah:

In the year that King Uzziah died I saw the Lord sitting upon a throne, high and lifted up; and his train filled the temple. Above him stood the seraphim; each had six wings: with two he covered his face, and with two he covered his feet, and with two he flew. And one called to another and said: "Holy, holy, holy is the LORD of hosts; the whole earth is full of his glory." And the foundations of the thresholds shook at the voice of him who called, and the house was filled with smoke. And I said; "Woe is me! For I am lost; for I am a man of unclean lips, and I dwell in the midst of a people of unclean lips; for my eyes have seen the King, the LORD of hosts!"

Then flew one of the seraphim to me, having in his hand a burning coal which he had taken with tongs from the altar. And he touched my mouth, and said: "Behold, this has touched your lips; your guilt is taken away, and your sin forgiven." And I heard the voice of the Lord saying, "Whom shall I send, and who will go for us?" Then I said, "Here I am! Send me." And he said, "Go, and say to this people: 'Hear and hear, but do not understand; see and see, but do not perceive.' Make the heart of this people fat, and their ears heavy, and shut their eyes; lest they see with their eyes, and hear with their ears, and understand with their hearts, and turn and be healed." Then I said, "How long, O Lord?" And he said: "Until cities lie waste without inhabitant, and houses without men, and the land is utterly desolate, and the LORD removes men far away, and the forsaken places are many in the midst of the land.[3]

The New Testament also contains references to a number of experiences that might be included in this category. I will cite two here. The first is the incident now commonly called the Transfiguration, which is reported in three of the Gospels. This account is that of Luke:

> Now about eight days after these sayings he [Jesus] took with him Peter and John and James, and went up on the mountain to pray. And as he was praying, the appearance of his countenance was altered, and his raiment became dazzling white. And behold, two men talked with him, Moses and Elijah, who appeared in glory and spoke of his departure, which he was to accomplish at Jerusalem. Now Peter and those who were with him were heavy with sleep but kept awake, and they saw his glory and the two men who stood with him. And as the men were parting from him, Peter said to Jesus, "Master, it is well that we are here; let us make three booths, one for you and one for Moses and one for Elijah"—not knowing what he said. As he said this, a cloud came and overshadowed them; and they were afraid as they entered the cloud. And a voice came out of the cloud, saying, "This is my Son, my Chosen; listen to him!" And when the voice had spoken, Jesus was found alone. And they kept silence and told no one in those days anything of what they had seen.[4]

The second account from the New Testament is one that I take from the opening chapter of the book of *Revelation:*

I John, your brother, who share with you in Jesus the tribulation and kingdom and the patient endurance, was on the island called Patmos on account of the word of God and the testimony of Jesus. I was in the Spirit on the Lord's day, and I heard behind me a loud voice like a trumpet saying, "Write what you see in a book and send it to the seven churches, to Ephesus and to Smyrna and to Pergamum and to Thyatira and to Sardis and to Philadelphia and to Laodicea."

Then I turned to see the voice that was speaking to me, and on turning I saw seven golden lampstands, and in the midst of the lampstands one like a son of man, clothed with a long robe and with a golden girdle round his breast; his head and his hair were white as white wool, white as snow; his eyes were like a flame of fire, his feet were like burnished bronze, refined as in a furnace, and his voice was like the sound of many waters; in his right hand he held seven stars, from his mouth issued a sharp two-edged sword, and his face was like the sun shining in full strength.

When I saw him, I fell at his feet as though dead. But he laid his right hand upon me, saying, "Fear not, I am the first and the last, and the living one; I died, and behold I am alive for evermore, and I have the keys of Death and Hades. Now write what you see, what is and what is to take place hereafter. As for the mystery of the seven stars which you saw in my right hand, and the seven golden lampstands, the seven stars are the angels of the seven churches and the seven lampstands are the seven churches.[5]

Finally, let me quote an autobiographical account from a much later Christian writer, St. Teresa of Avila, a sixteenth-century Spanish writer:

At the end of two years, during the whole of which time both other people and myself were continually praying for what I have described—that the Lord would either lead me by another way or make plain the truth: and these locutions which, as I have said, the Lord was giving me were very frequent—I had the following experience. I was at prayer on a festival of the glorious Saint Peter when I saw Christ at my side—or, to put it better, I was conscious of Him, for neither with the eyes of the body nor with those of the soul did I see anything. I thought He was quite close to me and I saw that it was He Who, as I thought, was speaking to me. Being completely ignorant that visions of this kind could occur, I was at first very much afraid, and did nothing but weep, though, as soon as He addressed a single word to me to reassure me, I became quiet again, as I had been before, and was quite happy and free from fear. All the time Jesus Christ seemed to be beside me, but, as this was not an imaginary vision, I could not discern in what form: what I felt very clearly was that all the time He was at my right hand, and a witness of everything that I was doing, and that, whenever I became slightly recollected or was not greatly distracted, I could not but be aware of His nearness to me.

Sorely troubled, I went at once to my confessor, to

tell him about it. He asked me in what form I had seen
Him. I told him that I had not seen Him at all. Then he
asked me how I knew it was Christ. I told him that I
did not know how, but that I could not help realizing
that He was beside me, and that I saw and felt this
clearly; that when in the Prayer of Quiet my soul was
now much more deeply and continuously recollected;
that the effects of my prayer were very different from
those which I had previously been accustomed to experience; and that the thing was quite clear to me. I
did nothing, in my efforts to make myself understood,
but draw comparisons—though really, for describing
this kind of vision, there is no comparison which is
very much to the point, for it is one of the highest
kinds of vision possible. This was told me later by a
holy man of great spirituality called Fray Peter of Al-
cantara, to whom I shall afterwards refer, and other
distinguished and learned men have told me the same
thing. Of all kinds of vision it is that in which the devil
has the least power of interference, and so there are no
ordinary terms by which we women, who have so little
knowledge, can describe it: learned men will explain it
better. For, if I say that I do not see Him with the eyes
either of the body or of the soul, because it is not an
imaginary vision, how can I know and affirm that He
is at my side, and this with greater certainty than if I
were to see Him? It is not a suitable comparison to say
that it is as if a person were in the dark, so that he
cannot see someone who is beside him, or as if he were

blind. There is some similarity here, but not a great deal, because the person in the dark can detect the other with his remaining senses, can hear him speak or move, or can touch him. In this case there is nothing like that, nor is there felt to be any darkness—on the contrary, He presents Himself to the soul by a knowledge brighter than the sun. I do not mean that any sun is seen, or any brightness is perceived, but that there is a light which, though not seen, illumines the understanding so that the soul may have fruition of so great a blessing. It brings great blessings with it.

It is not like another kind of consciousness of the presence of God which is often experienced, especially by those who have reached the Prayer of Union and the Prayer of Quiet. There we are on the point of beginning our prayer when we seem to find Him Whom we are about to address and we seem to know that He is hearing us by the spiritual feelings and effects of great love and faith of which we become conscious, and also by the fresh resolutions which we make with such deep emotion. This great favour comes from God: and he to whom it is granted should esteem it highly, for it is a very lofty form of prayer. But it is not a vision. The soul recognizes the presence of God by the effects which, as I say, He produces in the soul, for it is by that means that His Majesty is pleased to make His presence felt: but in a vision the soul distinctly sees that Jesus Christ, the Son of the Virgin, is present. In that other kind of prayer there come to it influences

from the Godhead; but in this experience, besides receiving these, we find that the most sacred Humanity
becomes our Companion and is also pleased to grant
us favours.

My confessor then asked me who told me it was
Jesus Christ. "He often tells me so Himself," I replied;
"but, before ever He told me so, the fact was impressed upon my understanding, and before that He
used to tell me He was there when I could not see
Him." If I were blind, or in pitch darkness, and a person whom I had never seen, but only heard of, came
and spoke to me and told me who he was, I should
believe him, but I could not affirm that it was he as
confidently as if I had seen him. But in this case I could
certainly affirm it, for, though He remains unseen, so
clear a knowledge is impressed upon the soul that to
doubt it seems quite impossible. The Lord is pleased
that this knowledge should be so deeply engraven
upon the understanding that one can no more doubt it
than one can doubt the evidence of one's eyes—indeed, the latter is easier, for we sometimes suspect that
we have imagined what we see, whereas here, though
that suspicion may arise for a moment, there remains
such complete certainty that the doubt has no force.[6]

You will remember that in the first chapter of this book, I
tried to draw a distinction between *claiming* that something is a fact—for example, that it is a fact that I can speak
English—by asserting the corresponding proposition, and
*manifesting* or exhibiting that fact by making it accessible

to someone else's experience. I may claim and assert that I can speak English without manifesting that fact, because I can assert the appropriate proposition in some other language. On the other hand, I can manifest my ability to speak English by actually speaking in that language, even if the topic about which I speak has no reference to my linguistic abilities. And, of course, I may manifest many facts, including many facts about myself, without resorting to speaking at all.

Now, as the title of this chapter suggests, I intend here to focus primarily on the ways in which we may think of God revealing something by manifesting it—that is, by His making the corresponding fact accessible to human experience—rather than by His communicating it—that is, by His asserting that it is a fact. In the actual religious texts, however, and especially in those that are strongly influenced by a Christian orientation, the two modes of revelation tend to be combined. I think that is not something that we need to find surprising, but I will postpone what I have to say about its significance until the next chapter. Here however, I will ignore, as much as possible, the elements of God's speaking, and similar references to linguistic activity in these accounts.

While there is this distinction, there are also some close affinities between the manifestation and communication models, affinities that make it possible for us to make some observations that apply to both of them. Both of them, for example, invite us to consider the relevance of the "secular" uses of the terminology of revelation.

In fact, the notion of revelation does not seem to be

uniquely religious. Or, to put it in the formal mode of speech, the noun "revelation" and the verb "to reveal" seem to have perfectly idiomatic uses in linguistic contexts that are about as non-religious as any context can be. So it seems perfectly idiomatic to say, for example, that the attorney revealed that she was employed by the CIA, or that this piece of information was one of the revelations that came out of the trial. These words, then, do not seem to belong to a special religious vocabulary; they belong rather to that great bulk of terms in our language that can be used in both religious and non-religious contexts.

For our purposes, this fact embodies both an advantage and a danger. The advantage is that we can conduct at least part of the analysis of the concept of revelation by looking at the secular uses of the relevant terms. These uses are less likely than the religious uses to stir up in us immediately some deep-rooted disagreements, and thus they are less likely to divert us initially from the purely analytic task of clarifying a set of meanings. The danger is that there might after all be something special and important about the religious sense, something that we might miss, or perhaps even reject, if we concern ourselves too much with the secular uses. I shall try to make some use of the advantage without, I hope, falling prey to the danger.

We can also, I think, make use of a single schema for formulating revelation claims of both the manifestation and the communication variety. At least, I will propose a schema of that sort and will explore some of its utility. The schema I propose is as follows:

(S) $m$ reveals $\alpha$ to $n$ by means of (through, etc.) $k$.

The instantiation for $m$ I will call the revealer, or the agent of the revelation; $\alpha$ represents the content of the revelation, and $n$ the recipient; $k$ represents the mode or means of the revelation.

Strictly speaking, this schema is not complete. It would come closer to being complete if, for example, it also included variables for time and place. I do not know what would be required to make it fully complete. In (S), however, I have included those elements that seem to be most significant and interesting.

With the possible exception of $k$, I take all of the elements in (S) to be *obligatory*, in the following sense. If there is an actual and genuine revelation then there is some true proposition that has the form of (S), and in which each variable has been replaced by an appropriate individual constant. This does not imply, of course, that we cannot properly refer to a revelation by asserting a proposition that provides less information than (S) calls for. We can sometimes, for example, generalize over some of these variables. Or we may simply leave out any reference to one or another of the items in (S). Those items are obligatory only in the sense that, if there is a genuine revelation, then there must in fact be instantiations for those variables.

I referred above to "appropriate" replacements for these variables. We can make some progress in understanding the idea of revelation by reflecting further on what would be appropriate in one case or another. For example, what sorts of individuals are appropriate as instantiations for $m$? This is, of course, a question about what sorts of things can reveal something, or—going again to the formal mode of speech—what sorts of things can appear as subjects of the active or reflexive verb "to reveal" or as subjects of a "by" phrase after the passive forms of that verb. Persons come to mind first, and they certainly form one important class of revealers. But situations and impersonal entities—even inanimate objects—are also said to reveal. Think, for example, of sentences like "The footprints revealed that one of the travellers was a child" and "The depth of their interest is revealed by the fact that not one of them bothered to come."

In religious contexts God is usually, no doubt, thought of as the revealer and He is generally made the subject of the corresponding sentences. There are, however, religious revelation claims, even within a Christian context, that do not, ostensibly at least, have God as their subject. So we might say that the Bible reveals that . . . , or that the destruction of Jerusalem revealed that. . . . Many religious people, however, would take such sentences as equivalents of the claims that God revealed something through the Bible, or by allowing the destruction of Jerusalem, and so on. And there seems to be a good bit of plausibility in this contention. Notice however, that the parallel claim about the secular uses would not be plausible. "The footprints revealed that one of the travellers was a child" is not plausibly taken to be equivalent to any statement to the effect that some person revealed, by or through the footprints, that one of the travellers was a child. I have not been able to think of a clear case of a religious revelation claim that is not plausibly convertible into a claim that God revealed something.

This may suggest that in its religious use this concept is limited to, or at least very strongly inclined toward, a single subject, that is, God.

Moving on to the next item, what can we put into (S) in place of α? That is, what sorts of thing can be the content of revelation? Theologians who accept and use the concept of revelation in their work often involve themselves in disputes over what it is that is revealed. Some of these disputes, of course, involve alternatives that, we might say, belong to the same category. So some theologians might debate as to whether the doctrine of the pre-millennial return of Christ has been revealed, rather than some incompatible doctrine, such as perhaps post-millennialism. But I have in mind here those disputes in which the alternatives seem to belong to quite different types, and in which, indeed, the debate emphasizes the difference in type. So it is not uncommon now to read that modern theologians favor the view that in revelation God reveals Himself, while earlier theologians are said generally to have held the view that God revealed a set of truths, propositions, or doctrines.[7] And this difference is often thought to represent an important change—usually, indeed, it is represented as a major improvement—in the theological understanding of revelation. Can the secular sense of revelation throw any light on this debate?

Well, one version of the question of what can be revealed is the formal mode question of what sorts of things can properly appear as direct objects in sentences whose main verb is an active form of "to reveal," and what sorts of things can properly appear as subjects of the passive and reflexive forms of "to reveal." But at least in the secular contexts the answer must surely be "many very different sorts of things." In the first place, persons can be revealed. So, for example, "The eavesdropper revealed himself by stepping out from behind the draperies" seems to be a perfectly straightforward sentence, and it says that, by performing a certain action, a certain person revealed *himself*. But propositions—or, what are curiously difficult to distinguish from true propositions, facts—are also readily said to be revealed, as in the case of the attorney who reveals *that she is employed by the CIA*. And things that are neither persons nor propositions also fit perfectly well. The parlor magician may open his hand and reveal an egg instead of the coin that we expected, and a person may reveal her insecurity by glancing repeatedly at the door. We could therefore say that if the secular uses of this term are a reliable guide to its religious sense, than the question of what category of thing has been revealed by God is not likely to be settled by reference to the notion of revelation itself.

We could perhaps go further by noticing that a single agent, in a single context, and by means of a single act, can reveal several things of widely disparate categories. So the eavesdropper, when he steps from behind the drapery, may with equal propriety be said to reveal *himself*, to reveal *his presence*, and to reveal *that he is there*. And if we do not care to choose between these we need not do so. There is nothing either logically or pragmatically queer about a single person's asserting all three of these things about the eavesdropper. In the same way the person who glances nervously at the door may reveal both *her insecurity* and *that she fears someone will enter the room.* And so on. Evidence, therefore, that in a certain situation a thing of a certain category has been revealed need not always be taken as evidence that nothing of any other category has there been revealed. To return to the theological case, we might have reason to believe or to say that in a certain act or situation God had revealed Himself. We should not, however, be too hasty to take that as a reason for refusing to believe or to say that in that very same act God had revealed some proposition or doctrine.

In (S), the variable *n* refers to the recipient of the revelation. A revelation of either the manifestation or the communication variety would seem to be a species of experience. If the revelation is genuine at all, then it is a conscious and at least partly cognitive encounter with an entity external to the self. Ordinary sense experiences, such as seeing a brick wall or tasting a lemon are, as James noted, our stock examples of objective experiences. But what kinds of experience there are I take to be itself a matter of experience, and hence I do not accept a prior restriction of the notion of experience to the simply sensory.

Even if revelation is a species of experience, not every experience seems to be a revelation. But I am unsure as to how to differentiate the notion of revelation in general from the wider notion of experience. Perhaps if we limited ourselves to the religious case the matter would be simpler. At one time I believed one could distinguish revelation from experience in general in terms of the intention of the "object," that is, the agent of the revelation. But there is some reason, to be discussed shortly, to think that this will not work for all cases. Perhaps it is on the right track anyway, and we should treat the recalcitrant cases as secondary and derivative.

At any rate, if I am correct in thinking that a revelation is a sort of experience, then the appropriate substitutions for $n$ must refer to individuals that are capable of having experiences. This would require, I suppose, that they be entities that are capable of consciousness and cognition.

In my schema, $k$ refers to the means by which the revelation is accomplished. It isn't very hard to think of examples of this element. "The eavesdropper revealed his presence by stepping out from behind the draperies" seems straightforward enough. And some religious people might say, for example, that God revealed His anger over the sins of Judah by permitting the destruction of Jerusalem. I shall have a little more to say about some revelatory means, especially in the final chapter.

I suggested above, however, that possibly $k$ is not obligatory. This is the possibility that some revelations are a sort of divine "basic act," something that is done by the divine agent, but not by His doing something else. At present I don't know anything very decisive for or against that possibility.

That brings us to the end of the variables in (S). But I want to add here some observations about these topics that are closely related to what we have just been saying.

The first of these concerns the relation of revelation to

intention. I have sometimes said myself that the notion of a revelatory experience differs from that of experience in general by including an element of intention and purpose on the part of the thing that does the revealing. This cannot be correct, however, for all of the uses of the revelation terminology. For the footprints do not intend to reveal that one of the travellers is a child, nor does that situation seem to require that anyone have that intention. On the other hand, we might wonder whether revelation requires the intention of the revealer when the revealer is a person. This would not be trivial. Persons can do many things without intending to do those things or even any closely related thing. It might be important to notice, if it were a fact, that revealing is something that a person cannot do unless he intends to do it, or perhaps unless he intends to do some related thing. Unfortunately this suggestion does not seem to work either. For the person who reveals her insecurity by glancing at the door may not intend to reveal anything at all.

Nevertheless, there remains something attractive about the suggestion. By examining some footprints we might discover that one of the travellers is a child, and we might therefore say that the footprints reveal . . . and so on. By examining some people we might discover that Hansen's disease is endemic in the Philippines. But there is something not quite right in saying that these people had revealed that Hansen's disease was endemic in the Philippines. A person who said that would normally be taken to mean that the people had *said* that Hansen's disease was endemic. So perhaps there is something special about persons as revealers after all. My suspicion is that in some way the notion of revelation is linked specially or primarily with persons and with intentional acts, and that other uses are derivative. But for the present I must leave this matter unclear.

The second point concerns the relation between revelation and truth. It can be put most easily for those cases in which what is revealed is a proposition, but it has its analogues for the other revelational objects also. For the propositional case it is put briefly by saying that revelation involves truth. It is put perhaps more precisely by saying that statements of the form "$n$ reveals that $p$" entail $p$. This is not, of course, to say that no revelation claim may involve a falsehood, nor that a person may not believe to have been revealed a proposition that is actually false, and so on. I am simply saying that when it is claimed that a certain proposition has been revealed that claim is not true unless the proposition itself is true. (But, of course, I am not saying that the entailment holds in the other direction, that is, that a proposition's being true entails that it is revealed.)

I believe that this is a fairly clear feature of the ordinary uses of the revelation terminology, a feature that is shared with a number of other important epistemological concepts, such as knowledge and proof. The most common evidence that we do normally recognize this sort of entailment is the way in which we refuse to use the revelation terminology in those cases in which we do not believe the associated proposition. If the attorney says that she was employed by the CIA, and we believe her then we might say that she revealed that she was employed by the CIA. If we do not believe her—if we think she is lying or even if we are merely in some doubt—I think we would not normally speak of her revealing something. Rather we would talk of what the attorney *says,* or *claims,* or *asserts,* or *argues,* and so on. For unlike the notion of revelation none of these latter notions is specially attached to truth.

The epistemological concepts that involve truth give rise to the so-called "pragmatic" paradoxes. Thus, there is something queer about someone's saying something like, "Professor Plushbottom knows that *p,* but I, on the other hand, do not believe that *p.*" There is, of course, nothing at all queer in the *situation* that such a proposition describes or asserts to be the case. That is, there is nothing queer about one person's knowing a proposition that another person does not believe. Indeed, the statement, as uttered by a particular person—Professor Milquetoast, say—may well be true. For Plushbottom may know that *p* and Milquetoast may not believe that *p,* and that is just what the statement asserts to be the case. Nevertheless, there is something queer, "pragmatically" paradoxical, about Milquetoast's making such a statement even if it is true. And one way of getting at that queerness is in terms of the queerness of Milquetoast's saying that Plushbottom knows that *p* when he himself does not believe that *p.*

In a similar way there are the pragmatic paradoxes of revelation. "The Bible reveals that Jesus will come again, but I do not believe that he will come again" is paradoxical in this way, as is "The footprints revealed that one of the travellers was a child, but I do not believe that there were

any children among them." Again, the situations asserted
to be the case may actually obtain. But the person who says
such things cannot be taken to be speaking both correctly
and straightforwardly. One immediately senses the disap-
pearance of the tension if he considers replacing these sentences with "The Bible *says* that Jesus will come again,
but . . . ," and "The footprints *suggested* that (made it appear as though and so on) one of the travellers was a child,
but . . . ." And all of these are indications of the internal
connection between the notions of revelation and truth.

We have to notice, of course, that for the revelation terminology, as also for knowledge, proof, and the other epistemological notions that involve truth, we have another
sense as well. We might call these the "ironic" senses of
these terms, and we normally use some special linguistic
sign to call attention to these ironic uses and to assure that
they are not mistaken for the normal uses. In writing,
quotation marks around the crucial word are the most
often used device. In speaking we may apply to it a special
and striking intonation, or accompany its utterance with a
"knowing smile," a wink, or some other gesture. So one
could, in the proper context and in the proper way, write or
say, "Despite all that has been said on the subject, old
Plushbottom still 'knows' that the circle can be squared. In
fact, he is quite prepared to prove it!" And we can write or
say that, in this ironic way, without committing ourselves
to the claim that the circle can be squared. But the fact that
we feel impelled to use special quotes, intonation, or something when saying such a thing is itself an indication that
the curcial words are there being used in a queer and ab-

normal way. I have no doubt that we can use "reveal" and its cognates in a similar ironic way. No harm is done by that, I suppose, if we do not confuse such occasions with more ordinary ones.

So far, we have been talking of the way in which this feature of revelation appears when its object is a proposition. It isn't hard to see how it applies to other cases, though a comprehensive statement of the relations might be hard to frame. If a person reveals her insecurity then she must really be insecure (not merely appear to be insecure), if the magician opens his hand and reveals a real egg where we had expected a coin, then there must be a real egg in his hand, and so on. If we agree on the propositional case then probably no great difficulty will arise over these other cases.

Finally, there is the way in which revelation is person-relative. This is a feature that revelation shares—so it seems to me, at least—with both proof and knowledge. If something is known, then there is someone who knows it; if something has been proved, then (on my view, at least) there is someone to whom it has been proved;[8] and if something has been revealed it seems natural to suppose that there is someone to whom it has been revealed. Furthermore, the fact that a certain person knows something, or has had something proved to her, or has had something revealed to him, does not seem to entail that everyone else, or even anyone else, knows that thing, or has had that thing proved to him, or has had that thing revealed to him. That set of features belonging to certain epistemological terms, including these three, I call person-relativity.

But now consider these assertions:

(1) Professor Plushbottom knows that $p$, but I do not know that $p$.

(2) That $p$ was proved to Professor Plushbottom, but it was not proved to me.

(3) That $p$ was revealed to Professor Plushbottom, but it was not revealed to me.

Assertion (1) strikes me as queer and paradoxical in a way in which (2) and (3) do not. If a person is willing to claim that someone else knows something then it is natural to expect him to be willing to make that same claim for himself with respect to that proposition, and it would be queer, perhaps paradoxical, if he were not willing to do that. But that is not so for proof, nor for revelation. One can ascribe these to other people, relative to a certain proposition, without claiming them for oneself (and, of course, vice versa).

But consider also

(4) That $p$ has been proved to Professor Plushbottom, but I do not know that $p$.

(5) That $p$ was revealed to Professor Plushbottom, but I do know that $p$.

These are queer too, much like (1). But of course neither (1), (4), nor (5) is a self-contradictory or necessary falsehood. On the contrary, these paradoxical assertions might be perfectly true.

The case of (1) does not seem to involve much difficulty. A person who is in a position to assert the first conjunct of (1) is in an equally strong position to assert $p$ itself. And such a person is in an equally strong position to assert that he knows that $p$. So when he denies that he knows that $p$ the paradox arises. But the conjunction is not self-contradictory because a person can assert what he is not "in a position" to assert (and vice versa), and he may assert truths even though he is not "in a position" to assert them. So (1), though paradoxical, may be true.

The case of (4) and (5) is similar. Since the notions of both proof and revelation involve truth, a person who is in a position to assert the first conjunct of (4) and (5) is in an equally strong position to assert $p$ itself. So she is in a position to assert that she knows that $p$, and if she denies that she knows that $p$ she speaks paradoxically (though perhaps truly).

Put in a somewhat different way, proof and revelation are ways of knowing. A person can have a way of knowing that $p$ only if $p$ is true. Consequently, if I know that some other person really does have a way (for example, proof or revelation) of knowing that $p$ then I myself must have a way of knowing that $p$ is true. And so it would be queer for me to assert (4) or (5). But though I must have some way of knowing that $p$ I need not have the *same* way of knowing as this other person. So it would not be queer for me to assert (2) or (3).

Like knowledge, then, revelation is person-relative in that the fact that something is revealed to one person does not, in general, entail that it is revealed to someone else. Unlike knowledge, it is also person-relative in the sense that a person may know that something has been revealed (to someone else) without its being the case, in general, that it has been revealed to her.

Let me end this chapter now with a speculation about a way in which a revelation in the manifestation mode may be more fundamental in revelational theology than a communication-type revelation. It is sometimes suggested that no one could acquire the belief that there is a God by divine revelation (or perhaps that no one could *properly* acquire it in this way). For the knowledge, or belief, that there is a God is a prerequisite to receiving a revelation, or (so to speak) for squeezing the cognitive juice out of the revelatory orange. And this is, I think, one of the reasons—maybe one of the main reasons—for thinking that some sort of natural theology is a necessary preliminary to any sort of revealed theology.

On certain views of revelation this claim makes some sense and is quite plausible. Locke, as you may remember, claimed that in the case of revelation one accepted the revealed content "on the credit of the proposer." The Lockean scenario of revelation seems to be rather straightforward. It has an analogue, for example, in the way in which I sometimes read the *Encyclopedia Britannica*. In the Lockean picture of revelation, one receives a putative piece of information, and knows that it came from God. (For the moment, never mind how either of these things happens.) But, so far as truth is concerned, one is prepared to give God a lot of credit. As Locke says somewhere, He can neither lie nor be mistaken. (Perhaps, indeed, God's line of credit is unlimited.) And so one accepts the putative infor-

mation as the truth, a revealed truth. But it seems plausible
to suppose that if one did not already believe that there was
a God, and that He was a reliable source of truth, then one
would not be able to carry this scenario out to its conclusion.

The Lockean scenario is intended, I think, to apply to the
communication model of revelation. In fact, that may be
the only way in which Locke thought of revelation: it was
just God's speech, and nothing else. And a notion like that
of the "credit of the proposer" seems especially appropriate
to that model. When someone tells us something, then our
readiness to believe it is often a function of a judgment that
we make about the reliability of this informant. I say that
this notion is especially appropriate to the communication
model; whether it is fully appropriate is something that we
may explore a little further in the final chapter of this book.
Here, however, it is important to notice that the idea of the
"credit of the proposer" has little (if any) relevance to a
revelation construed as a *non-communicative* manifestation. When the eavesdropper reveals his presence by stepping out from behind the draperies, when the heavily
bearded gentleman reveals that he is bald by removing his
hat in the elevator, then my belief that there is an eavesdropper present, or that the man is bald, does not seem to
require any special judgment on my part about their "credit" or credibility. It looks as though the facts toward which
my beliefs are oriented are simply manifested in a way that
makes them available for my perception and apprehension,
and that's all there is to it. In that way, taking off your hat

seems to be importantly different from saying, "You know, I'm bald as a cue ball," even if they tend to produce the same belief.

The line of argument that I sketched above, therefore—the argument that depends on Locke's scenario—would be ineffective against a person who claimed that the knowledge that God exists (or that there is a creator of the world, and so on) was derived from a divine revelation of the manifestation variety. For in a revelation of that sort the fact that is to be believed is manifested (presented, made available for apprehension, and so on) rather than being asserted. And so I know of no philosophical reason for thinking it to be impossible that a person's theological and religious knowledge might *begin* with revelation, and might be a revelational knowledge throughout, at least if it begins with revelation as manifestation.

To say that a person's religious knowledge might begin with revelation, however, should be taken to mean only that her first relevant piece of knowledge in this area is revelational knowledge. It should not be construed as denying that there is *something* that such a person must have before she has the revelation. It denies only that what is prerequisite to the revelation is itself a piece of knowledge or belief.

This point is closely related to a further question. If one is indeed to begin in this revelational way, and if indeed God does manifest Himself in some experience, then how is it that one recognizes the object of that experience as God? Even if we construe the content of the revelatory experience along some minimalistic lines, such as Gary Gutting's "core" of religion,[9] the conviction that there is someone (or something) out there that cares for us and for our welfare, how is that fact conveyed in the experience? What is it about the experience that warrants *that* belief? And if we think of the revelatory content in some richer way—that there is a creator of heaven and earth, say, or that there is a person who is omnipotent and wholly good—the question may seem even more puzzling.

You will remember that, in the passage that I quoted early in this chapter, Teresa of Avila seems to discuss some questions of this general sort. When she told her confessor that she had visions of Jesus he asked her how she knew that it was Jesus who appeared to her. And when she herself reflected on what she called a "non-imaginary" vision of Jesus—that is, a vision that involved no imagery of any sort—she asked herself how she came to know that Jesus was present, close to her, at her right side, and so on.

In the latter case, Teresa begins by comparing the case with that of being aware of another human being in a dark room. But, she says, they are not very similar after all. For she thinks that in the case of the human being, I must be proceeding on the basis of other sensory clues—the rustle of clothing, the sound of breathing, and so on. But in the non-imaginary vision there is, so she thinks, no imagery at all. So if she knows that Jesus is close beside her, at her right hand, on the feast day of St. Peter, she does not know it by having a visual image of him there, nor an auditory image, nor a tactile image, nor anything of the sort.

To the confessor who asks how she knows that it is Jesus,

she replies first that he often tells her so himself. But then she adds that sometimes she knows who it is without his telling her. How does she know? If I remember correctly, Teresa in one place describes a vision of Jesus in which, so she says, he looked just like the painting of him in a certain church. Evidently that was an imaginary vision, and perhaps Teresa thought (in that instance) that she recognized Jesus by his appearance, much as a policeman might recognize a suspect on the street after he has studied the photograph in the precinct station. But when she talked to her confessor after the feast of St. Peter, she did not give that sort of reply. The Jesus of the non-imaginary vision could not be identified by comparing him with his picture. So how does she know? Teresa says in effect that she knows that it is Jesus, but she does not know how she knows it.

If we are sympathetic to Teresa's claim at all, we might interpret it in at least two ways. Perhaps Teresa does have a way of knowing that it is Jesus, a way of recognizing him, but she just isn't able to describe that way in any satisfactory and illuminating manner. Maybe we are familiar enough with our own analogues of such a situation. All of us, for example, can recognize a lot of friends and acquaintances, but many of us cannot give a good description of our friends. Although we recognize our friends right off, as soon as we see them on the street, we may not be able to describe them well enough to enable a police officer to recognize them. Presumably we recognize our friend by noting such details as the shape of her nose, the angle at which she carries her head, the rhythm of her walking, and so on. But when we are called on to say just what those identifying details are, we may find ourselves at a loss. Perhaps that is Teresa's situation.

There is, however, a more radical interpretation of Teresa's reply, and one that is perhaps more in tune with the passage itself. On this interpretation, Teresa doesn't have any way at all of knowing that it is Jesus; she has no means of identifying him. But in saying this we must emphasize that on this interpretation (as I construe it anyway) we really do mean that she has no *way*, no *means,* of doing these things. This does not entail that she cannot do them. It entails that if she is to recognize Jesus then she must do so without a means of doing so. She must do it directly, not by doing something else. It must be, that is, a basic cognitive act.

Now, it seems pretty clear that there are many things that we do by doing something else. We are, I suppose, familiar enough with stock examples, such as my frightening the burglar by turning on the light. It seems plausible to suppose, however, that there are occasions in which I do something without performing an infinite series of prior acts as means to this final act. And that seems to entail that there are some things that I can do without having to do something else in order to do them. Probably I cannot turn on a light in that way; I can do it only by moving my hand, or some such thing. But moving my hand may be the sort of thing that I can do directly, and not merely by means of doing something else. (Of course, I can also move my hand by doing something else. I can, for example, use one hand to grasp the other and move it. The difference in the way in which I would be moving the two hands would illustrate the distinction that is involved there.) The acts that I perform without performing some other act as a means of performing the first are the basic acts.

Whatever plausibility attaches to the view that there are basic physical acts would seem to attach also to the claim that there are basic cognitive acts. No doubt, for example, I sometimes recognize the validity of some complex and arcane argument by analyzing it into a series of simpler arguments. But somewhere—for me, anyway—such analyses come to an end. I get to a point where I seem to recognize directly that a certain argument (or argument form), such as *modus ponens,* is valid. Just as in the case of physical actions, if there are not some cognitive acts that are basic, then it is hard to see how I could get started on the cognitive life at all.

What I suggest, therefore, is that we should construe Teresa's view as being that her recognition of Jesus in her non-imaginary vision was a basic cognitive act. It is an act that she has no *means* of performing, and therefore she cannot tell us how she performs it. Or at least, she *may* not be able to tell us how she does it. It is, nevertheless, an act that she can, and does, perform.

It would not follow that there was no explanation of any sort of how Teresa does such things. I can move my left hand. I can also move my left ear. But I can do one of these things as a basic act, while I cannot do the other one in that way. No doubt that is because of the great difference in the musculature and neural apparatus associated with the ear and with the hand. And most of that difference, I suppose, is innate. It is part of my original equipment as a physical animal. There are some things that this animal can do, and some things he cannot. And if the Christian view of creation is correct, then (I suppose) the physical capacities that I have in fact—and therefore what actions I can perform in the basic way—are largely due to the creation of God.

If Teresa, then, is to recognize God (or Jesus and so on) in some experience of the divine self-manifestation, and if her recognition is to be a basic cognitive action, then (I suppose) she must have a capacity for doing such things. And since I believe that she is one of God's creatures, it also seems plausible to me to suppose that this capacity, if she indeed has it, is part of His endowment to her.

# 4

## THE COMMUNICATION MODEL

I turn now to that model of divine revelation that probably comes first to mind for many of us, especially if we have been accustomed (as I have) to thinking of this topic from within the Christian tradition. It is the third, and last, of the models that I mentioned in Chapter 1, the one I call "the communication model." In this model the operative analogies and the terminology are drawn from the domain of speech and related linguistic activities. One thinks of God as speaking with men and women, as saying something to them; and these human recipients, for their part, are represented as the hearers of the word of God. (I think that a secondary, though important, feature of this model is the construal of God as Himself a hearer of human speech, as one who listens to human prayer and responds to it. But I will not say much here about this complementary element.) Because we are so likely to think of speech, and similar linguistic activities, as idiosyncratic to persons, this way of thinking of revelation is especially prominent in religions—such as Christianity—that construe God as being a person or something very much like a person. It fits much less comfortably with the non-theistic types of religion.

Judaism, Christianity, and Islam have often been known as "religions of the book." I think that they are religions of the book because they were first, and more basically, religions of the word. That is, they were religions of the *divine* word, representing themselves as the recipients of a divine revelation conveyed by God's speaking to, and through, prophets. Buddhism on the other hand, though it has a corpus of written sacred texts much more extensive than that of Christianity, does not seem to be nearly so much a religion of the book, or of the word. For (as I understand it, anyway) the Buddhist texts are thought of as being *about* religious matters, but not as emanating *from* the divine reality as a communication.

This explains too, I think, a fact that we noted in the preceding chapter, the fact that in the biblical literature even those experiences that seem to be the best candidates for manifestation revelations tend to include a large element that belongs to the communication side of the picture. That is, visions and similar events in which it would seem plausible to say that there was being manifested something like the glory of God, His majesty and power and so on, also normally include an element of God's speech or something similar. In fact, I think, that element tends to give these accounts a more "natural" feel. The interaction between persons normally has a strong tendency to include an element of speech. The idea of two persons encountering each other in any profound way without talking to each other is likely to strike us as strained, odd in some way. It could happen, of course. But we would wonder what was the matter with them, what special constraint barred them from the more normal modes of personal interaction. (Even anger and enmity are often expressed in speech.) If we are accustomed to thinking of God as a person, or as something very much like a person, and if we can think of a divine-human encounter at all, then we will also find it natural, I believe, to suppose that some sort of divine speech will be an important element there.

These same elements are formalized and ritualized, I think, in the pattern or liturgy of many traditional church services. In those services some elements—the prayers and perhaps also the hymns—are thought of as a human speech addressed to God, while a different set of prominent elements—the reading of the Scriptures and the preaching of the sermon—are construed as the occasions on which the worshippers hear God speaking to them.

The biblical literature of Christianity, in both the Old and New Testaments, seems to me to be just full of this notion of divine revelation. Almost everywhere in that literature one runs into the idea of God's speaking, of the word of God, of what God has said or is saying, and so on. It would not be implausible to suggest that the idea of a communication-type revelation is the most prominent special epistemological idea in the biblical literature.

It seems to me, in fact, that in the biblical literature the idea of the word of God is sometimes carried well beyond the areas of communication and revelation. In the early chapters of Genesis, for example, God is represented as creating the world by speaking. He *says,* "Let there be light," and there is light. And in the first chapter of the Gospel of John the divine person who becomes incarnate as Jesus the Christ is described as the Word of God, the *Logos* who was with God and who was God from the beginning. But these more "metaphysical" elements in the biblical idea of the divine word will not play much of a role in my discussion here. I will instead concentrate on the idea of a divine communication.

My strategy for the remainder of this chapter is roughly as follows. I will say something first about the possibility, as it appears to me, of such a mode of revelation. Then I will consider briefly a variety of miscellaneous points that often give rise to misunderstandings in thinking about revelation in this way. I will then close the chapter with a somewhat more extended discussion of two topics: one of them involves the ways in which such communications could generate human knowledge, and the other involves a special kind of mediation that I think is often involved in this mode of revelation.

Could there be a divine revelation of this sort, a speaking in which God is the speaker and human beings are the hearers? If there is no divine person then there could not be any such revelation. If there is no divine entity at all then there can be no divine revelation of any sort. And if there is a divine entity, but not one who is a person or something very much like a person, then (while perhaps there could be a revelation of the manifestation variety) there could not be a divine speaking. Or so, at least, it seems to me. People, therefore, who believe that there exists nothing of the required sort—no God—will naturally be correspondingly skeptical about claims that there have been communications from God. We can hardly blame them for that latter skepticism. But that skepticism will be largely, if not wholly, a reflection of their prior atheism. We need not treat it as if it had *independent* grounds, at least not until such grounds are produced. If we do not share the atheism, therefore, and do not find some compelling reason to do so, then we need not think that divine communications are *ab initio* impossible.

Some people, I suppose, may have more theologically based reasons for rejecting the idea of a divine communication to human beings. It may be suggested, for example, that it would be beneath the dignity of God to engage in such an interchange. Or it might be thought that a divine speaking would somehow infringe on human autonomy. With respect to the first suggestion, I will not speak at all for other religions. But the complaint there made seems to me to belong to a family of complaints that have been made against Christianity from the beginning. After all, the Incarnation itself is beneath the dignity of God as that dignity is sometimes construed. Christianity must simply live with that objection, insisting that this *a priori* idea of what the divine dignity consists in must be rejected and replaced with an alternative idea that itself grows out of the things that God actually does in the world. If God becomes incarnate, then so much the worse for the sort of dignity that would preclude that humbling, and if God in fact speaks to men and women, then again so much the worse for any conception of the divine nature with which such speaking in incompatible.

The other objection mentioned above, involving human autonomy and so on, may perhaps best be considered in connection with one of the miscellaneous points below.

Some who have no general philosophical or theological objection to the possibility of a divine communication may nevertheless have doubts as to whether there has ever in fact been any such revelation. Against this doubt we could set the testimony of many people that there have indeed been such revelations, and that they have been the recipients of some of those revelations. I believe many such testimonies to be the truth, but it is not part of my project here to prove that this is a fact. For a reason that I shall try to explain later, I think that such a project is not likely to be useful.

Perhaps we can do something useful, however, by trying to clear up some misunderstandings, and by getting a better positive understanding of what would be involved in a revelation of the sort here being considered. I turn, therefore, first to the miscellaneous points I mentioned earlier.

In the preceding chapter I proposed a general schema for revelation claims: $m$ reveals $\alpha$ to $n$ by means of $k$. Would the communication model be identified by something special that goes into the instantiation of this schema? I think it would, but perhaps in a way that turns out not to be very interesting. I think that it will not be identified by the instantiations for $m$ and $n$. In *every* mode of divine revelation $m$ will be God, and for every mode that is addressed to human beings *n* will, of course, be one or more human beings. The instantiation for α might give us a clue, because α might be the sort of thing that we think *could not* be revealed other than by communication; it could not, for example, be manifested. If there are such revelational contents, and if we could identify them, then we might thereby have reason to think that a certain revelation (if it occurred at all) must have been in the communication mode. But for the most part, I think that if the communication mode is identified at all within my schema that identification will occur in the instantiation for *k*. When we come to say *how* God revealed α, then we will say that He did so by *saying* α, by *telling* us something, and so on. In a similar way, if we want to identify the manifestation mode, then we will most likely do so by saying that God revealed something—His glory, for example—by *manifesting* it, by showing it forth, or something of the sort. And in the case of the causation model, a person who is inclined to think along the lines of Plato or Descartes, or maybe of Calvin, might say that God had revealed something to him by *implanting* that knowledge or belief in him at his creation.

The modes of revelation, that is, seem to me to belong to the category of ways in which God does reveal, or might reveal, something. If that is correct, however, then we should also recognize that having identified such a mode we might want to ask again about how that mode was implemented. It might be that God has revealed what will happen at the end of the world by telling somebody about it. But we might still want to ask how it was that God spoke to that person. There is not bound to be only a single possible answer to that question, and I want to say more about it later on. For now, however, we can note that in my schema $k$ (perhaps unlike the other variables) can be instantiated more than once, and at different levels.

In some moods, Christians who take the idea of revelation seriously, and particularly the idea of a communication from God, are likely to think of the content of revelation primarily in terms of information. They often put this point by saying that they insist on the reality of propositional revelation, that is, of a revelation whose content consists of propositions. I too believe that there is indeed a divine propositional revelation, and that this revelation is important to Christianity. But we should note that propositional revelation is not uniquely linked with the communication model, and also that the Christian tradition certainly seems to recognize non-propositional contents within the divine speaking.

We have already noticed, in the preceding chapter, that it seems to make perfectly good sense to specify a propositional content for a manifestation-type revelation: remember, for example, the man who reveals that he is bald by taking off his hat in the elevator. If we could specify the content of a certain divine revelation as consisting of one or more propositions, then, that would not by itself guarantee that this revelation should be construed along the lines of the communication model. Propositional revelation and the communication model of revelation are not linked in a one-to-one fashion.

Propositions can be revealed in ways other than by communication. Can something other than propositions be revealed by communication? Yes. Or perhaps the answer is "yes" if we can stretch the concept of revelation in still another dimension. In the story of the initial human fall in Genesis, God is represented as speaking to Adam and Eve and asking them a question: "Who told you that you were naked?"[1] And somewhat later He is said to have asked Cain, "Where is your brother Abel?"[2] And still later, in the Abraham/Isaac story, God is represented as commanding Abraham to sacrifice Isaac.[3] In all of these stories, and in many others in the biblical literature, God is represented as speaking. But in these particular cases, the content of the divine speech is not a proposition but something else, a question or a command. And that would be a point of similarity between the divine speech and human speech. For our speaking too includes many speech acts other than the asserting of propositions.

In fact, the contents of some of these other sorts of acts—questions, for example, and commands—seem to be much more closely tied to the notion of speaking than are propositions. We have already noticed that it seems quite possible to reveal a propositional content without anything like speech, simply by making manifest the fact that the proposition would express. But it is much harder, to say the least, to imagine how one could do something like that with a question or a command if one had no linguistic resources at hand. Could we, for example, make any sense out of the Abraham/Isaac story (whether construed as history or as fiction) if we did not include in it God's ability to speak? I suspect that we could not.

People often ask questions, of course, because they have a desire to learn the answer to that question; that is, they want to come to know the information that the question seeks to elicit. And they often issue commands, or make requests, in order to obtain the corresponding state of affairs. That a person wants to know a certain thing, or wants to have a certain thing done, is itself a fact about that person. There is a proposition that expresses that fact. And that proposition, so far as I can see, could be revealed, either by communication or in some other way. But revealing the fact that I want to know a certain piece of information, or that I would like to have a certain thing done, is not the same thing as asking the corresponding question or issuing the corresponding command or request.

Perhaps the easiest way to see this is to notice that it often makes perfectly good sense to ask a question even if we do not want to learn the corresponding information, and it makes sense to issue a command even if we do not want to have the corresponding act performed. A teacher, for example, who asks a child, "Who was the first president of the United States?," probably does not want to learn who the first president was. Probably she already knows the answer to her own question perfectly well. Her question has a quite different purpose, but it is a legitimate question nevertheless. God asked Cain where his brother was, but it seems rather unlikely that God was trying to find out where Abel was. His question, too, had a different purpose. But it was a genuine question.

In a similar way, the ending of the Abraham/Isaac story suggests that God did not really want, or intend for, Abraham to carry out the sacrifice of Isaac. Nevertheless, God commanded him to do it. And it is not all that hard to think of human analogues of that strategy.

Questions and commands, therefore, cannot be construed simply as the equivalent of revealing a desire to know or to have something done. For there are straightforward questions and commands that are not correlated with such desires. And, going in the other direction, one can easily have a desire to know—even a burning desire—and nevertheless refrain from asking the corresponding questions. One may even reveal such a desire, perhaps inadvertently, and the person to whom that desire is revealed may satisfy it by providing the information, while it remains true that one has not asked the corresponding question. And similar observations may be made about commands and the desire to have a certain act performed.

It seems to me, therefore, that there is not much chance that the functions of such speech acts as questioning and commanding could be replaced by the asserting of propositions. That seems possible neither in the human nor in the divine case. If we take seriously, then, the possibility of a divine speaking to human beings, we should be careful not to think of it purely in terms of the asserting of propositions, or of the conveying of information.

Here, however, we run into another problem involving the concept of *revelation*, at least as it might be strictly construed. If God asserts some proposition, it seems natural enough to say that God revealed whatever information the proposition expresses. But it does not seem quite idiomatic to say that God revealed *Where is your brother Abel?* God *asked* Cain this question, He *said* to Cain, "Where is your brother?," and so on. But the verb "to reveal" does not seem to be really idiomatic when the content of what is said is a question. Nor, it seems to me, does it go really naturally with commands and requests.

I suspect that this is a terminological point without much deeper significance. If I am right about that, then we can resolve it in one way or another. We can stretch the term "revelation" a little beyond its common usage, and make it cover questions, commands, and perhaps even some other sorts of speech acts. Or we can leave the notion of a communication-type revelation pretty well tied to information and propositions, and then say that the divine speaking also involves other sorts of communication that are not revelation—such things as questions and commands. Here I will adopt the first alternative. But I have no objection to anyone who prefers the second.

If God does reveal propositions at all, then what sorts of propositions does He reveal? I suppose that most Christians who have taken seriously the idea of a propositional revelation have naturally been most interested in revelational contents that seem to have a profound theological or religious significance—such things, for example, as the nature of the Trinity, the significance of the Incarnation, the destiny of human beings after their death, the end of the world, and so on. I have no objection at all to the suggestion that God can reveal, and has revealed, information about some things of this sort. But it is a curious fact, and perhaps one of some significance, that in the biblical literature itself the speaking of God is not at all confined to matters of profound theological import or to otherwise impenetrable mysteries.

I do not mean here to be making the point that the Bible contains a large amount of information about "mundane" matters. That is certainly true, and it is a point to which I want to return shortly. But here I call attention to a somewhat different fact, the fact that the biblical literature sometimes represents God Himself as revealing, in his speech with human beings, information that is about as secular and mundane as one could imagine.

In the account of the investiture of Saul as the first king of Israel, for example, there is an interesting little story.[4] It is said that Saul (perhaps being nervous or bashful) went and hid, and was not to be found when the actual ceremony was to be performed. It is then said that the elders of Israel "inquired of the LORD," and that the LORD *said* to them, "He has hidden himself in the baggage."

Now, if there is any sort of information at all that belongs to the "ordinary" world, if there is any sort of fact that is "secular," then must not this be an example of it? It is, after all, just information about where a certain young man has gone to conceal himself (and he had not, in fact, gone very far, or concealed himself in any very ingenious manner). It is just the sort of thing that is the substance of a thousand routine police investigations every day, to say nothing of ten thousand exasperated searches by parents.

But the writer of this account apparently did not hesitate to ascribe to God Himself the revealing of this apparently mundane and secular information. There is often said to be such a thing as "revealed theology." The proposition that Saul has hidden himself in the baggage is not likely to be found as a doctrine in any such theological system. But, in the biblical account, it is one of the things that God is said to have revealed, or at least one of the things that God is supposed to have said.

A rather similar sort of case appears in the account of the life and work of one of Israel's great prophets, Elisha.[5] There it is said that God (apparently rather routinely) revealed time and again to Elisha where the Syrian army was preparing an ambush. Elisha was passing this information on to the king of Israel, who was then, naturally enough, avoiding the ambushes. And the Israelis were so successful in these maneuvers, according to this account, that the Syrian authorities came to suspect that their ranks had been infiltrated by a high-level spy.

Of course, some people may not be very ready to take these stories at face value. I am inclined to do so myself, but maybe that is not very important here. However we construe them—historically, mythologically, fictionally—they represent a certain way of thinking of divine revelation. And that way accepts the possibility that such a revelation need not be restricted to matters of high theology, the arcane mysteries of the inner life of God, or any such thing. God can also speak, if He wishes, even about Syrian soldiers. And perhaps He does so wish.

This is, no doubt, a way of thinking of the divine action that is not "spiritual" enough to satisfy some intuitions about God. According to these intuitions, God ought not to concern Himself with such things as these. (We might remember that Aristotle says that God will think only about the best thing—that is, about thinking itself—and that there are some things that it is better not to know than to know.)[6] And even if He happens to know such things He certainly ought not to bother Himself with revealing them to human beings. Let Him leave military intelligence to the Israeli staff, and let the elders of Israel make their own search for Saul.

This sort of objection is, I think, closely related to one I considered earlier. It proceeds from a certain conception of the divine majesty, the divine dignity, or perhaps in this case, of the divine spirituality. But maybe these intuitions are themselves somewhat off the mark. For what if it turns out that God is just not as spiritually minded as are some theologians? That seems to me, at least, to be a real possibility. Perhaps such things as battles, and the investiture of a minor king, and even the question of where to find a coin to pay the local tax collector, are things in which God takes an interest. And perhaps it is not beneath the dignity of God to reveal such things also to those who need to know them. At least, I cannot think of a clear reason for supposing that these are not possible contents of divine revelation. And the biblical tradition seems to take them for granted.

It is also sometimes suggested, I think, that a propositional revelation from God would somehow damage human autonomy, intellectual freedom, or something of the sort. (And it is also sometimes suggested that a divine pronouncement about morality would be fatal to moral autonomy.) It is hard for me, at least, to get up much steam over this objection, because it seems to me to construe human autonomy in such an unrealistically fragile manner. The human will, one would think, would be blown to bits by the gentlest breeze. The facts, however, seem to be quite otherwise. Human stubbornness (or determination, if we prefer) seems capable of almost incredible exploits of resistance. Perhaps, indeed, God's omnipotence could in the end overbear all human efforts. But if there is anything at all in the Christian idea of the ways in which God actually undertakes to speak to human beings and to reveal Himself to them, then these divine efforts seem to be routinely resisted. That God speaks to someone, even expressing some proposition, does not at all seem to guarantee that what He says will be accepted.

Even in those cases in which the divine word is accepted and believed, there seems to be no appreciable damage to human autonomy and initiative. Perhaps if God were to reveal *every* fact in which a person were interested, then some other natural human activities would be inhibited. Maybe, for example, such a person could not engage in independent research, or some such thing. And perhaps that would be a serious loss. But it does not at all follow that God's revealing of *some* information need have that consequence. No one, after all, supposes that the autonomy of chemists is damaged by the fact that they normally read the labels on their reagent bottles. For their research usually does not consists of analyzing those reagents, but rather of using them to analyze something else. That chemists can generally rely on the information given on the labels, in fact, enables them to spend their time and effort on more interesting investigations. It thus enhances their initiative, rather than hindering it. Even in the purely theological realm, I would suspect that human thought and creativity is more likely to flourish than to be stifled if it is nourished by a genuine and living word of God.

According to the account in Genesis, God asked Cain, "Where is your brother Abel?" But, so far as I know, God has never asked *me* where Abel is. Indeed, that question would not make much sense if directed to me, since I have no brother at all. God may also have commanded Abraham to sacrifice his son Isaac. That command was not directed to me, and it would not make much sense if it were, since I have no son, Isaac or otherwise. Of course, God may be asking me about *someone* for whom I ought to have some concern, or He may be commanding me to do something, or even to sacrifice something. But He is not asking me about Abel or commanding me to do something about Isaac.

In these cases it is fairly easy, I think, to see that there must be a sort of person-relativity about the divine speech. Not every command can reasonably be thought to be addressed to me, even if I happen to know about it, and not every question can be addressed to me. I believe that we ought to recognize a similar person-relativity in those cases in which the divine speech involves the conveying of information.

We can begin with purely human cases. Perhaps North told Poindexter, and Poindexter told Weinberger, and Weinberger told Regan, and Regan told the President. Let us imagine that in this little scenario everyone believed what he was told, or even that he came to know the information contained in these reports, something that he did not previously know or believe. My scenario implies, of course, that *someone* told the President. But my description would not normally be taken, I think, to suggest at all that it must have been North who told the President. It certainly does not *require* that interpretation. The someone who did tell the President, according to my story, is Regan, and it need not be anyone else. It may, of course, be true that if North had not told Poindexter, then no one would have told the President. North's original revelation may have been essential to the rest of the events. But that need not make North the agent of those later events.

I believe that we should make a similar distinction with respect to the divine revelation of information. There may, indeed, be some information that God reveals to everyone. But I see no reason at all to assume that whenever He reveals *anything* He must reveal it to everyone. Perhaps God really did reveal to Elisha just where the Syrians had laid an ambush. In order to believe that, I need not believe that God must also have revealed that same information to the wine merchants of Athens (nor, for that matter, to me). And there may, of course, be a reason for revealing something to one person and not to another. It is not difficult to think of some plausible candidates for such reasons.

As we have seen in the purely human scenario above, the fact that a person's belief in some proposition is traceable, perhaps through many steps, to some other person's revelation of the information expressed by that proposition, does not entail that the original revealer revealed that information to the ultimate believer. I can see no good reason for thinking that a similar thing could not happen in the case of a divine revelation. For all I know, a divine revelation may have introduced some piece of knowledge into the intellectual patrimony of the human race, and that information may now be propagated to new recipients of it by one or another human means, without those people being themselves hearers of the divine speech. Maybe, indeed, God intended it that way.

In saying this, I do not intend to deny that there may be mediation in the process of revelation, nor even that something may be divinely revealed through *human* mediation. Purely human communication, and the sort of revealing that ordinary human beings accomplish among themselves, normally involves mediation. There is, after all, usually a *how* of it. It may be done by making vocal sounds, or by using the sign language of the deaf, or by writing, or by availing oneself of electronic technology, and so on. Perhaps there is also, at least sometimes, a *how* of the divine communication. God too may avail Himself of intermediates in His speech with human beings. And maybe sometimes these intermediates are themselves human beings.

(After all, God is often said to have spoken *through* prophets.) I turn now to that general topic.

The communication model invites us to think of revelation in terms of a divine speaking, or something like that. But I suppose that, if we are prepared to take this seriously as a possibility, we can hardly avoid wondering just how such a speaking is to be construed. In what way might God speak to human beings?

I said earlier that the communication model of revelation seems to be strongly prominent in the biblical literature. The revelation of God is there continuously described and reported in terms that suggest that God is thought of as speaking to men and women, thus communicating information to them, giving them commands and instructions, questioning them, and so on. But despite this prominence, there is, it seems to me, surprisingly little in the biblical literature about the phenomenology of this sort of revelation, about the *how* of divine communication, about what the receiving of such a revelation is like from the recipient's point of view. Of course, we need not restrict ourselves entirely to biblical material in thinking about this question, but for those of us in the Christian tradition it is a natural place to begin. And we may be surprised, or disappointed, in how little we seem to find there, at least at first sight.

It is not, however, that there is nothing there at all. For one thing, some revelational incidents, as they are reported in the biblical writings, appear to involve auditory perceptions, presumably much like those that are involved in the hearing of ordinary human speech. That seems, to me at

any rate, to be the most natural way to interpret reports
such as those of Isaiah's vision in the temple (Isaiah 6),
Moses and the burning bush (Exodus 3), Peter's rooftop
vision (Acts 10:9–16), much of the material in Revelation,
and some others. Part of the plausibility of this interpretation derives from the fact that in some of these cases the
recipients say that they "heard" a voice, or some such thing
(for example, Acts 10:13, Revelation 1:10, 4:1). Perhaps
even more suggestive is the fact that in many of these cases
the elements that best fit the communication model are em-
bedded within a broader manifestation, most often a "vision," in which other perception-like experiences, usually
visual, are prominent. In a context in which the human
subject is already represented as undergoing quasi-perceptual experiences of other sorts, it is natural to interpret a
reference to the divine speech as also involving a quasi-
perceptual auditory experience.

I refer here to these experiences as "quasi-perceptual" to
provide a more or less neutral way (epistemically neutral,
that is) of allowing that they may differ from "ordinary"
perceptual experience in some interesting and significant
way. To be more specific, these experiences may involve auditory sensations that are not correlated with the usual corresponding physical events—for example, atmospheric
sound waves and the like.[7] And while these experiences
may well be correlated with some neural events (perhaps in
the brain) that would accompany a similar "ordinary" auditory experience, they may also be lacking in *some* elements of the usual neurological machinery. If, for example,

the auditory sensation is produced without atmospheric vibration, then it would not be surprising if it were also lacking in any excitation of the auditory receptors in the inner ear.

As I understand it, it isn't all that unusual for some people to have auditory sensations in the absence of the usual physical stimuli (or to have visual sensations without the usual stimuli, and so on). Such experiences are often categorized as "hallucinatory." I believe that many such experiences are indeed hallucinatory, but I also suspect that not all of them are. The difference, as I see it, is that the notion of a hallucinatory experience involves a negative judgment about the veridicality of the experience, about the way in which that experience puts us into epistemic touch with a reality beyond ourselves, about the reliability of the experience if it is taken at face value. So the hallucinatory snake of delirium tremens is not a *real* snake (though of course the experience itself is a real experience), and the experience is not a reliable way of getting in touch with the reality of snakes in the world. The delirium tremens experience is indeed lacking in some of the usual physical correlates that go with a veridical perception of a snake: I suppose, for example, that there is no snake-like image cast upon the retina of the percipient's eye. And it may be the lack of these correlates that saps the experience of most of its epistemic force and reliability. But in saying that it is *hallucinatory* we focus primarily on its lack of epistemic veridicality, its lack of connection with a real snake that it appears to present for apprehension, and not upon its lack of such things

as a retinal image. Or that, at least, is how the word "hallucinatory" strikes me.

In the case of the person who "hears" something that
presents itself as the voice of God, however, I am not at all
ready *ab initio* to stigmatize her experience as non-ver-
idical, as lacking in connection with the reality that it appears to present. Maybe it *is* indeed the voice of God that
some people hear, God in very truth speaking to them. And
it would be misleading, at best, to call such experiences
"hallucinatory." That is why I have wanted to have a more
epistemically neutral term, one that would allow for the
possibility that these experiences may not have all of the
usual correlates of ordinary auditory experiences without
committing us to a negative judgment about the epistemic
significance of those experiences.

There appear to be, however, experiences that are reported as hearing the voice of God, or some such thing, but
that do not involve any auditory imagery, or indeed any
sensory imagery whatever. Teresa of Avila describes a
"non-imaginary" vision in which, as she says, "I saw Christ
at my side—or, to put it better, I was conscious of Him, for
neither with the eyes of the body nor with those of the soul
did I see anything."[8] Later on, in talking with her confessor, she says that this was not very much like apprehend-
ing the presence of a person in the dark, for in the latter
case one might "hear him speak or move." But in the case
of this vision, she says, "there is nothing like that. . . . He
presents Himself to the soul by a knowledge brighter than
the sun."[9] It would appear, then, that in this case the appar-

ent speaking of Christ was not accompanied by any auditory imagery.

Perhaps the speech element in this vision belongs to the class of experiences that Teresa elsewhere calls "locutions." In this sort of experience, she says, "though perfectly formed, the words are not heard with the bodily ear; yet they are understood much more clearly than if they were so heard, and, however determined one's resistance, it is impossible to fail to hear them."[10] I suppose that she here intends to describe a sort of cognitive experience that is like that which accompanies the hearing of human speech; there is, that is, a sequential apprehension of words, phrases, sentences, one after another, along with the corresponding sequential understanding of the information they convey, the questions they express, and so on. But this understanding and apprehension, though like that which ordinarily accompanies auditory sensation, occurs in this case without any such auditory imagery. And this would be the auditory analogue of Teresa's "seeing" that Christ was present, at her right hand, and so on, even though there was, as she says explicitly, no visual imagery at all.

Probably some of the biblical incidents belong to this general category. Maybe, for example, this is not an implausible interpretation of the "still, small voice" of 1 Kings 19:12. And perhaps at least some cases of the oft-repeated formula, "the word of the LORD came unto me," as it appears in the prophetic books, refer to an experience of this sort.

It strikes me as unlikely, however, that these sorts of cases exhaust even the biblical accounts. What else might there be? Well, for one thing, there might be cases that are, at least from one point of view, more complex than these. There is, for example, the story of the dream of the Pharaoh of Egypt, and the subsequent interpretation of that dream by Joseph.[11] Joseph prefaces his interpretation by saying, "God has told Pharaoh what he is going to do." I would myself find it natural to say that God spoke to the Pharaoh in, or by, this dream, or perhaps in the combination of the dream and its interpretation. At the very least, this revelatory incident, if it has any reality at all, fits the communication model better than it fits either of the others that we have considered. But if it really is a case of God's speaking to the Pharaoh, then the phenomenology of that speaking seems to be more complex than that of the cases we have so far considered.

Thomas Hobbes says somewhere that the claim that God has spoken to one in a dream amounts to no more than the claim that one has dreamed that God spoke to him. I believe that the epistemology of Hobbes' thesis is mistaken. But here it is more to the point to recognize that Hobbes' phenomenology seems also to be flatly in error. At least in the case of the biblical dreams that are represented as being associated with divine revelations, they are not characteristically dreams about God at all, either speaking or not speaking. In fact, I can't think of a single biblical dream to which any revelational significance is attached in which God appears as a dream character. And He certainly does not appear in the Pharaoh's dream, which is just about cows and wheat. Perhaps God speaks in, or by, or through, this dream, but it is plainly not a dream about God speaking.

I say that the phenomenology of this revelation seems to be more complex than in the cases earlier considered. If there is anything at all that God has revealed to the Pharaoh in this incident, it would seem to be something like "There will be seven years of good crops in Egypt, followed by seven years of crop failure and famine." Now, Joseph utters words to this effect in putting forward his interpretation of the dream. Is it possible that Joseph's utterance of these words, or his expression of this information, in some way constitutes *God's* communication of this information to the Pharaoh? Or might it be that the combination of the dream and Joseph's speech constitutes that communication?

In ordinary human speaking, communication takes place by way of some medium. In many cases the mode of communication is largely that of producing audible speech sounds. But of course that is not the only mode of human communication. We have writing, for instance. ("I heard from my friend today" need not imply that something was audible.) We also have the sign language of the deaf, signal flags, radio-transmitted Morse code, and so on. The Joseph story suggests that there may be a divine communication that utilizes as its medium the combination of a dream and its verbal interpretation by a human interpreter. If we are to rule this out, then at least we ought not to do so merely on the ground that this introduces some intermediation into the communication. For our most characteristic examples of human communication themselves clearly involve mediation. The mediation in the Joseph case would perhaps be more complex, and unusual or even unique. Must that rule it out of court?

Perhaps we ought not to confine ourselves, in this connection, to the case of Joseph and his interpretation of the Pharaoh's dream. Earlier in this chapter I mentioned the incident in which it is said that God told the elders of Israel where Saul had gone to hide. Nothing is said there about *how* God is supposed to have said this. We may, perhaps, imagine various possibilities. It could be, I suppose, by way of something like the sort of "locution" that Teresa describes. Or an experience in which the elders have the auditory sensation of hearing an audible voice enunciating a Hebrew sentence expressing that information, but with no human speaker of that sentence in the vicinity. Is it possible, however, that what happened on that occasion was that some child, playing in the baggage dump, had seen Saul sneaking in there to hide and then, when he heard that the elders were looking for Saul, said to them, "He's hiding down there where the baggage is"? Could that count as *God's* saying to the elders of Israel, "He has hidden himself in the baggage"? Perhaps it could. Perhaps it did.

In a paper on the significance of "Christian experience," William Alston lists a number of kinds of experience that seem to him to belong to "leading the Christian life." "We sometimes feel the presence of God," he says, "we get glimpses, at least, of God's will for us; we feel the Holy

Spirit at work in our lives, guiding us, strengthening us, enabling us to love other people in a new way; we hear God speaking to us in the Bible, in preaching, or in the words and actions of our fellow Christians."[12] The last clause of that sentence, which describes ways in which we "hear God speaking to us," makes a suggestion that is much like that of my preceding few paragraphs. It asserts that we hear God's speech to us, and that this speech is mediated in some complex way by such things as the Bible, Christian preaching, and the words and actions of other believers.

Almost fifty years ago John Baillie had suggested very much the same thing, but in a more extensive way, in his book *Our Knowledge of God*. Much of Baillie's exposition is autobiographical. He tries to reconstruct his own entrance into, and growth in, the life of faith. He begins the book by saying:

> The great fact for which all religion stands is the confrontation of the human soul with the transcendent holiness of God. When God reveals Himself to man, then a characteristic disturbance is set up in the human soul and in the life of our human society, and that disturbance is what we mean by religion. It is a disturbance of which we have all had some experience. Not one of us has been left alone by God. Not one of us has been allowed to live a purely human life with complete peace of mind.[13]

He goes on then to say:

> No matter how far back I go, no matter what effort of memory I attempt to reach the virgin soil of childish

innocence, I cannot get back to an atheistic mentality. As little can I reach a day when I was conscious of myself but not of God as I can reach a day when I was conscious of myself but not of other human beings. My earliest memories have a definitely religious atmosphere. They are already heavy with "the numinous". They contain as part of their substance a recognition, as vague and inarticulate as you will, yet quite unmistakable for anything else, of what I have now learned to call the divine as a factor in my environment. I cannot remember a time when I did not already feel, in some dim way, that I was "not my own" to do with as I pleased, but was claimed by a higher power which had authority over me.[14]

And then he suggests the way in which he supposes that divine self-revelation to have been mediated and effected.

Clearly, however, my infant experience was determined for me, to an extent to which it is difficult to set a limit, by the long tradition in which I stood. I was born into a Christian home, and God's earliest disclosure of His reality to my infant soul was mediated to me by the words and deeds of my Christian parents.[15]

Much later in the book Baillie returns to this theme. His account is so perceptive, it seems to me, that it is worth quoting at some length:

What I must do is to ask myself how the knowledge of God first came to me. And here I can only repeat what was said in the opening pages of this book: unless my analysis of my memory is altogether at fault, the knowledge of God first came to me in the form of an awareness that I was "not my own" but one under authority, one who "owed" something, one who "ought" to be something which he was not. But whence did this awareness come to me? Certainly it did not come "out of the blue". I heard no voice from the skies. No, it came, without a doubt, from what I may call the spiritual climate of the home into which I was born. It came from my parents' walk and conversation. At the beginning it may have been merely the consciousness of a conflict between my mother's will and my own, between what I desired and what she desired of me. Yet I cannot profess to remember a time when it was merely that. I cannot remember a time when I did not already dimly know that what opposed my own wilfulness was something much more than mere wilfulness on my mother's part. I knew she had a right to ask of me what she did; which is the same as to say that I knew that what she asked of me was right and that my contrary desire was wrong. I knew, therefore, that my mother's will was not the ultimate source of the authority which she exercised over me. For it was plain that she herself was under that same authority. Indeed it was not only from my parents' specific demands on me that this sense of authority same to me but from the way they themselves lived. Clearly they, too, were under orders, and under essentially the same orders. I cannot remember a time when I did not already know that what my parents demanded of me and what they knew to be demanded of themselves were in the last resort one and the same demand, however different might be its detailed application to our different situations. I cannot remember a time when I did not know that my parents and their household were part of a wider community which was under the same single authority. Nor again, can I recall a time when I did not know that this authority was closely bound up with, and indeed seemed to emanate from, *a certain story.* As far back as I can remember anything, my parents and my nurses were already speaking to me of Abraham and Isaac and Jacob, of Moses and David, of God's covenant with the Israelites and of their journey through the wilderness, of the culmination of the story in the coming of Jesus Christ, God's only Son, whom He sent to earth to suffer and die for our salvation; and then of the apostles and martyrs and saints and "Scots worthies" whose golden deeds brought the story down to very recent days. And I knew that that story was somehow the source of the authority with which I was confronted. I could not hear a Bible story read without being aware that in it I was somehow being confronted with a solemn presence that had in it both sweetness and rebuke. Nor do I remember a day when I did not already dimly know that this presence was God.

It was, then, through the media of my boyhood's

home, the Christian community of which it formed a part, and the "old, old story" from which that community drew its life, that God first revealed Himself to me. This is simple matter of fact. But what I take to be matter of fact in it is not only that God used these media but that in using them He actually did reveal Himself to my soul.

For what I seemed to know was not merely that God had declared His will to my parents and that they in their turn had declared their will to me, but also that through my parents God had declared His will to me. The story told me how God has spoken to Abraham and Moses and the prophets and apostles, but what gave the story its power over my mind and imagination and conscience was the knowledge that "in, with and under" this speaking to these others of long ago He was also now speaking to myself. That God should have revealed Himself to certain men of long ago could not in itself be of concern to me now; first, because, not being myself privy to this revelation, I could never know for sure whether it were a real or only an imagined one; second, because mere hearsay could never be a sufficient foundation for such a thing as religion, though it might be well enough as a foundation for certain other kinds of knowledge; and third, because the revelation would necessarily lack the particular authorization and relevance to my case which alone could give it power over my recalcitrant will. What is it to me that God should have commanded

David to do this or that, or called Paul to such and such a task? It is nothing at all, unless it should happen that, as I read of His calling and commanding them, I at the same time found Him calling and commanding me. If the word of God is to concern me, it must be a word addressed to me individually and to the particular concrete situation in which I am standing now. This insight into what we may perhaps venture to call the necessary "here-and-nowness"—the *hic et nunc*—of revelation is one which has emerged very strikingly from recent theological discussion.[16]

There are several elements in this account that are worth noting and summarizing.

First, as I have already said, this is an autobiographical account, a "testimony." It is Baillie's report of what his own experience seems to him to have been. But it is not by any means limited to a report of the purely "inner," or psychological, aspects of that experience. Like most reports of experiences, especially reports of experiences that do not seem to be notably religious, it unabashedly makes use of "objective" notions: the experience is described as being an apprehension of God, and God is said to be the source of it. An experiential report of this sort is not "incorrigible." That is, it is not bound to be correct. But more of that later.

Second, Baillie couches his report in terms of the self-revelation of God.

Third, this revelation is said to have been mediated by such things as the life of his parents and of the Christian community of which they were a part, and by the telling of the "old, old story." This latter is a reference to the Gospel, and to the associated biblical narratives, but Baillie adds that some non-biblical stories (for example, tales of the "Scots worthies," and even some accounts that had no obvious Christian content) also had a similar revelational significance.

Finally, Baillie seems to make a special point of denying that what happened was merely that he received, and accepted, reports of what God had done in other times and revealed to other people. It was *not* that God had spoken to prophets in an earlier age, and that an account of what God had revealed had been preserved, in the Bible or otherwise, so that Baillie could read it there and believe it. No, the Bible was certainly involved in what happened to him, maybe involved in some essential way. But what happened was not simply that Baillie believed that something had been divinely revealed to some other person. Rather, something was revealed *to John Baillie*. Put in terms of the schema that I introduced earlier, Baillie makes himself the instantiation for *n*, the recipient of the revelation. His own way of putting it is this: "But what I take to be matter of fact in it is not only that God used these media but that in using them He actually did reveal Himself to *my* soul."[17]

Is it possible that Baillie is essentially correct in the account he gives of his own experience?

This question can perhaps be "divided." Someone may wish to pursue the more general version of it, the question of whether it is possible for God to reveal Himself at all. I have already said a little about this version of the question. I will defer whatever else I have to say about it until later. Here, however, I want to consider the other (and more limited) version of the question about Baillie's testimony. Assuming that God can communicate with human beings in some way, could He communicate in the way that Baillie describes?

I said above that our most commonplace examples of communication involve intemediates of various sorts. It is, in fact, rather difficult to think of any clear case of human communication that does not pretty clearly depend upon mediation. (Perhaps the best candidate for an exception to this generalization would be the rather controversial possibility of telepathy.) It could hardly be plausible to object to the Baillie suggestion, therefore, merely on the ground that it involves mediation. If there is to be a viable objection it must refer to something special about the sort of mediation that Baillie claims.

One possible objection is cited by Baillie himself. He quotes Rousseau as asking, "Is it simple, is it natural, that God should have gone and found Moses in order to speak to Jean Jacques Rousseau?"[18] Perhaps the objection underlying this question could be put by saying the following: God *could* have revealed Himself to Baillie in some way other than this. There was, therefore, no necessity for Him to do it in this way. Therefore, He did not do it in this way.

To put the objection in this form, however, is to make it obviously implausible. For if this objection were to hold, then in any case in which God had available two or more ways of doing something, He could not do it in any way at all. But that seems absurd.

Perhaps, however, Rousseau meant to suggest something beyond this. Perhaps he thought that, if God were to speak to him at all, it would be *better* (simpler, more natural?) for Him to do it in some way that did not involve His first speaking to Moses. Any many of us have a strong tendency to assume that if God does anything at all, then He must do it in the best possible way.

Well, maybe God must indeed act in the best possible way. But that principle, even if it is true, must often fail to be of much use to us in settling questions like the one before us. For we are often not in a very good position to determine reliably which one of several alternatives would in fact be the best. Suppose that God could have spoken to John Baillie by a locution, or by an audible voice. Maybe that would have been simpler, as Rousseau suggests, than this other suggested mediation, which involves a prior divine revelation to Moses, the historical transmission of a record of that revelation, the apprehension of that record by Baillie, and God's use of that apprehension to convey His revelation now to Baillie. But assuming that the first alternative would have been simpler, what reason is there for supposing that it would have been *better*? Might it not be, as Baillie himself suggests, that the second alternative also has some special values of its own, such as contributing to an interrelatedness and unity of the people of God, both diachronically and synchronically? I, at any rate, have no great confidence in my own ability to determine the rel-

ative values of alternatives such as these—certainly not
enough confidence to overbear the force of a testimony
such as that of Baillie.

The Rousseau question, however, may suggest another
objection, or perhaps merely a possible misunderstanding.
God speaks to Baillie by first speaking to Moses. But how
does He speak to Moses? Must there not be somewhere a
way of the divine speech that does not require a previous
speech to someone else? So the Baillie suggestion could not
possibly be the whole story about the divine speaking.

I feel like agreeing with this observation immediately,
and observing that it does not constitute any objection to
the correctness of Baillie's understanding of what happened
to him. To say that this is what happened to Baillie does not
commit us to thinking that this is the *only* way in which
God can communicate with human beings. (In fact, only a
few pages back I suggested several other forms of mediation that such a communication might involve.) Saying that
this is what happened to Baillie does not even require us to
think that this is the *only* thing that happened to Baillie.

There is, however, also another direction that we might
explore. If we say that God spoke to Baillie by first speaking to Moses, then we raise the question of how He spoke
to Moses. Fair enough. In connection with the story about
Saul, however, I suggested that perhaps God spoke to the
elders of Israel by means of (or in, or through) some child's
telling them where Saul was hiding. But I did not suggest
that God had revealed this information to the child, or that
He had spoken to the child in any way at all. That account,

therefore, would not raise any question at all about *how* God had spoken to the child. And yet that account of how God might have spoken to the elders of Israel seems to have a lot in common with Baillie's story about himself.

Now, if there is anything at all that a person could come to know without divine revelation, then it would seem that information about where Saul was hiding would be a plausible example of it. I, at any rate, seem to find no difficulty in supposing that a child may well have observed Saul hiding in the baggage—observed him, that is, in the most ordinary human way. But if we can take seriously the possibility that God may reveal something to Baillie when he reads a story about Moses, or something written by Moses, then we can also, I think, take seriously the possibility that God may reveal something to the elders of Israel when some child tells them what he saw.

Now, Rousseau's question seems to assume an *iteration* of revelation, or at least that is one plausible way of interpreting it. It assumes, that is, that the medium of the later revelation is itself an earlier revelation. (That is what I have sometimes called a "parasitic" revelation.) But if the suggestion of the preceding paragraph is correct, then there might be a true account of a revelation that followed the general pattern of Baillie's account, but that did not refer to any previous revelatory event at all. Because this possibility does not require an iteration of references to revelation, it would seem to leave open the possibility that *all* of the divine speech might be complex in the way Baillie suggests for his own experience.

Another possible objection might go as follows. We can perhaps understand how a person could read the Bible, or hear a sermon, or even be told a story about a "Scots worthy," and how he could believe some, or even all, of the information contained in that story. Perhaps in that way a person could come to believe the Gospel; he could come to believe, that is, that the historical events of Jesus' life took place as they are described in the New Testament, and he might come to believe also that these events have the soteriological significance and so on that is there attributed to them. But this alone would not seem to satisfy Baillie. For he appears to insist that what happened was not merely his acquiring of this information. He insists that in this reading, hearing, and so on, *God was actually revealing Himself to Baillie*. And he seems to think that this is something special, something that is not common to every hearing or reading. For he suggests that there is some history that has no "presence" for him, in which he finds no sense of the divine speech addressed to him.[19] (And this is presumably not simply a matter of his not believing those accounts.)

But in that case, what is it that makes the revelatory reading and hearing special? Is this not a case of ascribing a difference that has no substantial basis?

I think that this is a deep question, and one to which I do not know any very detailed and illuminating answer. It seems to me that if there is indeed the difference that Baillie suggests, then something must be happening in the one case that is not happening in the other. I would suppose

that there must be in the one case some divine action that is
not present in the other. Many Christians do suggest that
there is a special action of the Holy Spirit, an "illumina-
tion" as it is sometimes called, that accompanies some of
our reading of the Bible, some of our hearing of the Gospel,
and so on. Perhaps that is the truth, and it is that divine
action that makes the difference between, on the one hand,
merely receiving and accepting a piece of information, or a
question, or something else, and, on the other hand, receiving a divine revelation. I myself believe that something like
this is probably the right account of the matter, but I do not
know much further to say about it.

A final objection. The complexity of this account, involving historical mediation, perhaps an iteration of revelations, and so on, seems to have no ready analogue in the
mediation involved in the paradigm cases of human communication. What reason, therefore, do we have to suppose
that Baillie is right in his account of what happened to him?
What reason, in fact, is there for supposing that it is even
possible that he is right about it?

I don't know whether it is really true that the complexity
of this account is unmatched in any more ordinary cases.
But I don't have any persuasive counter-example to put forward at present, so I will not contest that allegation very
strongly. Suppose it is as the objector says. What is the significance of that?

The truth is (it seems to me, at least) that we do not have
reliable *a priori* methods for determining what sorts of mediation will provide for the possibility of various kinds of

experience. Even in cases in which there has already been a large amount of empirical data collected, and in which there is already a substantial theoretical machinery for dealing with that data, there may yet be large areas of uncertainty. It is not all that uncommon, I understand, for an audiologist to be uncertain as to whether a certain type of hearing aid will substantially improve his patient's hearing before actually trying the device. If it doesn't work, well then the patient still doesn't hear. But if it does work, then the patient actually does hear the public lecture that he would not otherwise have been able to hear. Using the hearing aid, if it really works, does not merely enable one to acquire a certain body of information. It is not just the same thing as buying the *New York Times* and reading a transcript of the speech there. And it is not the same thing as having a friend give you a summary of the speech in a quiet room. What the hearing aid does, and what the *Times* does not do, is to enable one to *hear* the speech, and it enables one to hear *that speech,* and not merely some other speech about that one.

But the fact that a hearing aid does enable one to have these experiences is, it seems to me, a fact that we ordinarily learn (if we learn it at all) basically from our own experience or from the testimony of other people who claim to have some relevant experience. We do not ordinarily learn things of this sort merely by philosophical speculation. And I cannot think of any reason for expecting to learn, just by philosophical speculation, whether a human being can hear the divine speech in the way that

Baillie suggests. I have no *a priori* reason for thinking that it *could not* happen in that way. Of course, if I just had to sit around and invent a way for God to speak to human beings, perhaps I would not have invented this way. But then, probably I would not have invented a hearing aid either.

The testimonial feature of Baillie's account, therefore, seems to me to be both a strength and a weakness in it. Baillie claims that this is what actually happened to him. This is what his experience has seemed to him to be, from the inside, so to speak. So here we have not merely an abstract possibility, a pure speculation. We have instead a live human being who says, apparently in all sincerity, "This is what happened to me." That seems to contain within it the promise of some toehold on reality.

On the other hand, what we have in Baillie is largely *just* a testimony, along with (here, at least) the refutation of a few objections and the development of a few analogies. But it is possible for a person to be mistaken about his own experience, and for his own description of it to go astray. We do not have here a proof that Baillie is right about what happened to him. Is there anything that we do have, or that we could have, beyond Baillie's testimony?

I think that there is something that we could have, and that we might have, something that is better than that testimony, more solid somehow, richer in epistemic significance than any mere testimony can be. But Baillie cannot give it to us. That richer thing, which we could have and which perhaps we will have (or do have already), would be *an experience of our own.* If we ourselves never hear (or never recognize) the voice of God addressed to us, then I think that all that we have said so far must remain "merely" a speculation, a bare possibility at best. But if we do hear that voice, then we can make our own stab at saying how the divine speech has come to us.

In connection with a rather different sort of revelatory experience of her own, Teresa said, "If anyone thinks I am lying I beseech God, in His goodness, to give him the same experience."[20] It may be that this prayer is the best epistemic service that we can perform for one another.

# NOTES

## Chapter 1

1. See, e.g., Bruce A. Demarest, *General Revelation* (Grand Rapids, Mich.: Zondervan Publishing House, 1982), pp. 13–15.

2. C. S. Lewis, *Mere Christianity* (New York: Macmillan Co., 1956), p. 23 (Ch. 5).

3. Thomas Aquinas, *Summa Contra Gentiles*, Bk. I, Ch. 3.

4. John Locke, *An Essay Concerning Human Understanding*, Bk. IV, Ch. 18, Sec. 1.

5. *Ibid.*, Sec. 2.

6. Aquinas, *Summa Contra Gentiles*, Bk. I, Ch. 3, and *Summa Theologica*, Part I, Q. 1, Art. 1.

7. Locke, *Essay Concerning Human Understanding*, Bk. IV, Ch. 18, Sec. 4.

8. Alvin Plantinga, *God and Other Minds* (Ithaca, N.Y.: Cornell University Press, 1967), pp. 3–25.

9. Aquinas, *Summa Contra Gentiles*, Bk. 1, Ch. 3.

10. *Ibid.*

11. *Ibid.*

12. Ralph McInerny, "On Behalf of Natural Theology." in *Proceedings of the American Catholic Philosophical Association*, Vol. LIV (1980), p. 64.

13. Plantinga, *God and Other Minds*, p. 4.

14. Terence Penelhum, *God and Skepticism* (Dordrecht: D. Reidel Publishing Co., 1982), p. 96.

15. *Ibid.*, p. 98.

16. *Ibid.*, pp. 98, 99.

17. *Ibid.*, p. 97.

18. In 1970 I put forward a rather similar proposal myself in George I. Mavrodes, *Belief in God* (New York: Random House, 1970), pp. 29–35.

19. See e.g., his observations in Alvin Plantinga, *The Nature of Necessity* (Oxford: Clarendon Press, 1974), pp. 217–221.

20. Locke, *Essay Concerning Human Understanding*, Bk. IV, Ch. 19, Sec. 4.

21. See, e.g., Hans Kung, *Infallible?* (Garden City, N.Y.: Doubleday & Co., 1971).

22. Westminster Confession of Faith, Ch. 1, Sec. 6. The text of this confession can be found in John H. Leith (ed.), *Creeds of the Churches* (rev. ed.; Richmond, Va.: John Knox Press, 1973), pp. 192–230.


## Chapter 2

1. Plato, *Meno*, 85–86. The translation of the Plato passages is that of Benjamin Jowett (New York: Random House, 1937).

2. Plato, *Symposium*, 209–211.

3. *Ibid.*, 211.

4. René Descartes, *Meditations on First Philosophy*, Meditation 3. The Descartes selections here are taken from the translation of John Veitch (La Salle, Ill.: Open Court Publishing Co., 1962), p. 61.

5. *Ibid.*, pp. 49–51.

6. George I. Mavrodes, "Real and More Real," *International Philosophical Quarterly* 4 (1962): 554–561.

7. Descartes, *Meditations on First Philosophy*, pp. 49, 51.

8. Nicholas Wolterstorff, "Is Reason Enough?," *Reformed Journal* 31, no. 4 (April 1981): 22.

9. *Ibid.*

## Chapter 3

1. William James, *The Varieties of Religious Experience* (New York: Modern Library, 1902), pp. 67, 68 (Lec. 3).

2. *Ibid.*, p. 58.

3. Isaiah 6:1–12. The biblical quotations here are from the Revised Standard Version.

4. Luke 9:28–36.

5. Revelation 1:9–20.

6. St. Teresa of Avila, *The Autobiography of St. Teresa of Avila*, tr. by E. Allison Peers (Garden City, N.Y.: Image Books, 1960), pp. 249–251 (Ch. 27).

7. See, e.g., John Baillie, *The Idea of Revelation in Recent Thought* (New York: Columbia University Press, 1956), pp. 3–40.

8. I have discussed this somewhat more fully in George I. Mavrodes, *Belief in God* (New York: Random House, 1970), pp. 29–48. A similar view is advanced by Terence Penelhum, *God and Skepticism* (Dordrecht: D. Reidel Publishing Co., 1982), pp. 96–99.

9. Gary Gutting, *Religious Belief and Religious Skepticism* (Notre Dame, Ind.: University of Notre Dame Press, 1982), pp. 175–177.

Chapter 4

1. Genesis 3:11.

2. Genesis 4:9.

3. Genesis 22:2.

4. 1 Samuel 10:20–23.

5. 2 Kings 6:8–12.

6. Aristotle, *Metaphysics,* 1074b–1075a (Bk. XII, Ch. 9).

7. Cf. the curious account of the incident in which (apparently) some people report hearing the divine voice uttering a sentence, while others say merely "it thundered," in John 12:28–30.

8. St. Teresa of Avila, *The Autobiography of St. Teresa of Avila,* tr. by E. Allison Peers (Garden City, N.Y.: Image Books, 1960), p. 249 (Ch. 27).

9. *Ibid.,* p. 250.

10. *Ibid.,* p. 233 (Ch. 25).

11. Genesis 41:1–36.

12. William P. Alston, "Christian Experience and Christian Belief," in Alvin Plantinga and Nicholas Wolterstorff (eds.), *Faith and Rationality* (Notre Dame, Ind.: University of Notre Dame Press, 1984), p. 103.

13. John Baillie, *Our Knowledge of God* (New York: Charles Scribner's Sons, 1959), p. 3.

14. *Ibid.,* p. 4.

15. *Ibid.,* p. 5.

16. *Ibid.,* pp. 181–185.

17. *Ibid.,* pp. 183–184.

18. *Ibid.,* p. 185.

19. *Ibid.,* p. 186.

20. St. Teresa, *Autobiography,* p. 275 (Ch. 29).

# INDEX